Captain Rich No

Catchin'
Chesapeake Rockfish

Editors
RICH NOVOTNY
CYNTHIA NOVOTNY

Cover Design
BILL LAIDLER & JC GRAPHICS

Design & Typesetting
JC GRAPHICS

Photography
RICH NOVOTNY
JC GRAPHICS

Published in the USA by CS Publications.
1003 Foxridge Lane, Baltimore, Maryland 21221

First Printing March, 2004
Second Printing December, 2004

My Dad would say "I caught the biggest one"

 # Dedication

I'd like to dedicate this book to my Dad, Henry. He started me fishing when I was only six years old. He always took my brother Ron and I fishing with him in rented row boats, since we could not afford a boat of our own.

I can remember going to Wye Mills Landing or Queenstown and renting a row boat to go perch or bass fishing. I can still remember that six horsepower Wizard gasoline engine that started on at least the tenth pull of the starter cord. My Dad had the patience of a saint when it came to helping us fish. In those days we had conventional casting reels and my brother and I would get a backlash on at least every third cast. My Dad would give us his rod to fish while he straightened out our "*bird nests*" reel.

My Dad taught me a lot about fishing and becoming an adult. He taught me to be a good Catholic with high morals and values. He also taught me honesty and to respect my fellow man.

To this day he is my hero. Although he is only 5' 6" he still towers among men in my eyes. He is now 84 and I still look at him as my knight in shining armor. He has become my best friend in life as well as my first mate on the "*Oh Thank Heaven*". We have had some great moments while fishing together or just by being in each other's company. My Dad has the driest sense of humor that you can imagine. Everyone who has ever met my Dad enjoys his company and always ask about how he is doing the next time I meet them.

I love my Dad and I always greet him with a hug and kiss on the cheek or forehead and tell him that I love him. Remember to do this for your Dad since we won't have them with us all the time while we are on this good earth.

 **TABLE OF CONTENTS**

Fishing the *"Dumping Grounds"*

 **INTRODUCTION**

Throughout my 30 plus years of fishing for striped bass in the Chesapeake Bay, I have learned so much from so many individuals that I felt a real need to share this knowledge with everyone. I have given hundreds of seminars concerning fishing in the Chesapeake Bay and many fishermen have shown a keen interest in learning or improving their fishing skills. After each seminar or demonstration that I have given on fishing, quite a number of anglers have approached me and asked for more detailed information on some of the subjects that I discussed during my lecture.

Unfortunately, there are not too many books on the shelf that will give you detailed information concerning trolling, chumming, and

"Oh Thank Heaven"

eeling in the Chesapeake Bay. I hope that the information that I have provided in this book will help you better understand the art of fishing. Yes, as far as I am concerned, fishing is an art. Some may believe that fishing is merely throwing a hook or lure in the water and waiting for a fish to grab it. As you well know, this is not the case. Fishing requires techniques through trial and error or by going to the many seminars that are offered at boat and sport shows, or reading fishing articles in books or magazines. You could also join fishing organizations such as the Maryland Saltwater Sportfishermen's Association (MSSA) which invites expert guest speakers, to give fishing demonstrations at their local monthly chapter meetings sharing their individual fishing techniques.

I hope you will find this book interesting and beneficial for improving your fishing skills.

Captain Rich Novotny

 # STRIPED BASS (ROCKFISH) MORONE SAXATILIS

Morone saxatilis is the scientific name given to striped bass, better known as rockfish in Maryland. The East Coast stock of striped bass ranges from the St. Lawrence River in Canada through northern Florida. Striped bass are a long-lived species that have a life span up to 30 years.

The largest rockfish ever recorded weighed in at 125 pounds off of North Carolina in 1891. The current Maryland state record for a rockfish is 67.8 pounds and was caught by Devin Nolan. Devin was a 97 pound, seventh grader from Carroll County, when he captured this huge striper off of Bloody Point while fishing with his father. DNR fisheries biologist said the fish was approximately 23 years old and measured 52 inches in length with a girth of 30 inches.

Striped bass are an anadromous fish, which means that they leave the ocean to spawn in estuaries, bays or rivers, but remain in the ocean for most of their life. Spawning usually occurs during the spring from early April through May in Maryland. The Chesapeake Bay accounts for 70% to 80% of the composition of the East Coast migratory stock. Rockfish will stay in our estuary and river systems until the age of two or three. By this time, they are 12 to 16 inches in length. After their third year, a large percentage will 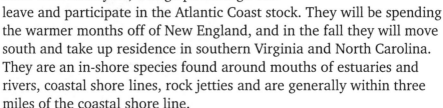 leave and participate in the Atlantic Coast stock. They will be spending the warmer months off of New England, and in the fall they will move south and take up residence in southern Virginia and North Carolina. They are an in-shore species found around mouths of estuaries and rivers, coastal shore lines, rock jetties and are generally within three miles of the coastal shore line.

Due to over-harvesting during the 1970's and early 80's a sharp decline of striped bass throughout its range occurred. Beside over-harvest, water pollution, acidic deposition and habitat destruction helped to exacerbate the decline. In the winter of 1984, the Maryland Saltwater Sportfishermen's Association (MSSA) sponsored a "*March on Annapolis*" with 800 recreational fishermen demanding that a moratorium be placed on rockfish. In 1985, after a threat of state rights pre-emption by the federal government, a moratorium on harvest was put in place by the State of Maryland.

Striped bass are managed federally by the Atlantic States Marine Fisheries Commission (ASMFC). Included in their fishery management plan are size limits, creel limits, seasonal closures and commercial landing quotas. The ASMFC controls fisheries that are in state waters which are within three miles of the shore. Other East Coast states complied with the ASMFC regulation and increased their minimum size limit to 38 inches, while Maryland was still under a moratorium. The reason for such a high minimum size was to protect the last strong "Young-of-the-Year" (YOY) class of 1982.

Devin Nolan and his 67.8 pound striper caught off of Bloody Point

Finally, after four years of poor spawning during the moratorium, a high level of spawning was measured in the Chesapeake Bay spawning reaches. Under the guidelines developed by the ASMFC, several criteria were established to cause for the reopening of the striped bass fishery in Maryland. The final criteria was met in 1989, when the striped bass juvenile index for that year was 25.2. ASMFC stated that Maryland's juvenile index had to have a three year running average of 8 to re-open the fishery. No one imagined that this high index number would happen in one year. In fact one of the lowest juvenile indexes occurred in 1990 - which was 2.1, while in 1988 the YOY index was 4.8 and in 1987 it was 2.7. Maryland has conducted this juvenile striped bass survey, better known as the *"Young-of-the Year"* survey since 1954. Maryland biologist designated 22 sites to seine for juvenile rockfish during July, August and September every year. At each site the number of juvenile rockfish are counted and recorded after two seine hauls at each of the 22 designated sites. The number of stripers are counted during the survey and then divided by the number of hauls to get the YOY index for that year. As you can see by the following chart, the index fluctuates dramatically from one year to the next.

MARYLAND DNR STRIPED BASS JUVENILE INDEX
Arithmetic Mean Catch Per Haul

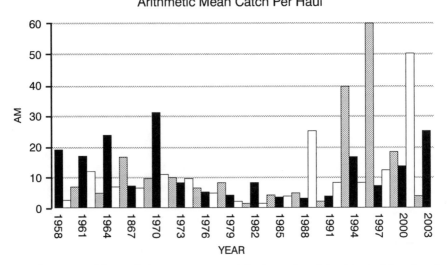

The striped bass fishery re-opened in Maryland in 1990. Maryland regulations call for the fishery to be divided into three categories. The allocation was divided at 42.5 percent for commercial fishing, 42.5 percent for recreational fishing and 15 percent for the charterboat industry. In 1990, the recreational fishery lasted only nine days as they caught their allocation of 318,750 pounds. In a report prepared by the Sport Fishing Institute, it states that *"Maryland anglers made an estimated 230,848 trips and harvested 381,367 pounds of striped bass during that short nine day season. These anglers spent an average of $55 each during their trip. The total economic output by these recreational anglers amounted to $22.3 million."*

Since the opening of the striped bass fishery in Maryland, we have enjoyed a much extended season since the stock was declared a restored stock in 1995. Since the start of the fishery we have been fishing under a harvest control model developed by Maryland's DNR. This harvest control model enabled Maryland fishermen to enjoy an extended fishery than most coastal states. For the 2004 season, we are allowed to possess stripers on the third weekend in April. We will be allowed one fish over a minimum size limit of 28 inches per day. Starting May 15th, our creel limit will go to two fish per day over an 18 inch minimum size limit. However, only one of the two can be greater than 28 inches. The recreational fishery will continue until December 15th of each year.

The striped bass recovery is truly a real success story when you think that the fishery was on the brink of disaster. It was accomplished by all East Coast states complying with the Federal Agency (ASMFC) stringent fishery management measures. We will now continue to reap the harvest of a robust fishery, thanks to their sacrifices.

My Dad trying to hold on to his trophy bass

GETTING READY FOR THE SEASON

It's the first of January and the temperature outside is 19 degrees and there is a foot of new fallen snow on the ground. Can you remember being on the water last spring battling that monster of a rockfish, as the sun warms your body in the 70 degree temperatures? Now the only thing to do concerning fishing is to watch ESPN on Saturday mornings and catch all of the fishing shows. Unfortunately, they show you places where they fish but you could never afford to go there yourself.

The next best thing is to begin to think about next year's fishing season. During the winter is the time to scrutinize your fishing equipment and tackle. Take an inventory of your lures, plastics, hooks and terminal tackle. The show season will begin soon, usually by the second week in January. From January through April, there are a number of boat and sport shows along with numerous flea markets. You will find some of the best bargains of the year at these events.

First, let's check our equipment. Inspect your rods to see if they are in good condition. Are all of the guides and reel seats in place and secure? Did you get that rod tip fixed that you broke last fall in the car door? Check your reels to see if they are working properly. Maybe you should break the reel down in order to apply new *"lube"* in the right places. You should change your line from last year. You don't want to lose that *"big one"* because of old, worn out line. Think about buying a heavier pound test line, maybe 17 to 20 pound line class for those spinning reels. Remember how close you were to other boats while eel fishing or drum fishing. Heavier test line will allow you the capability to bring the fish to the boat more quickly and avoid getting tangled with an angler on another boat. Change your line on your trolling reels as well. You have already made a big investment with the purchase of a rod and reel. Don't put off making a $12 to $20 purchase for new line. You should change your line on your reel every spring regardless of how many times you have used it during the previous season. You may even want to take some of your reels to the local tackle shop to let them service the reels before they break down during the season.

Let's take a look in your tackle box. Do you have enough terminal tackle such as snap and barrel swivels, three-way swivels, hooks of various sizes, sinkers, split shots, a good set of fishing pliers, de-hookers and leader line material? Now is the time to purchase these at the shows or at least the first part of the season at your local tackle shops. Remember during the season those racks start getting pretty depleted. While we are on the subject of tackle shops, try to support them whenever possible. Yes, you can probably buy something cheaper at the Wal-Mart or K-Mart stores, but your local tackle shop that sells you bait, cannot exist on just selling bait alone. Some of these tackle stores are open at 5:00 a.m. in the morning for your convenience. Have you tried to buy a bucktail or a landing net at 5:00 a.m. in the morning at K-Mart?

Next, inventory your lures that you will be using the entire year. For the spring fishery, do you have enough 8/0 to 10/0 bucktails, 8 to 20 ounce parachutes, spoons, umbrella rigs and a variety of plastics? I can't say this enough; you can get some great bargains at shows and flea markets; so stock up for the entire year. You can never buy too much since these items never go bad. This even pertains to buying lead sinkers.

When is the last time that you looked at your landing net? It is still in good shape or has it frayed over the past year? Is your net large enough to handle those 30 to 40 inch rockfish that were caught by anglers last spring or fall?

Are you planning to fish with eels or chum during the season? If so, it would be a good idea to construct a couple of live boxes for your eels. It's easy! Get a five-gallon bucket with a lid and drill plenty of small holes (smaller than the size of eels) in the bucket. Remove the wire handle and replace it with a nylon line. Tie it off of your pier or boat slip and you can keep eels alive all year. There is no need to try to feed them since they will feed on whatever is in the water. I know this for a fact because I left a dozen eels in my bucket all winter and didn't check them until April when I put my boat back into the water. All but two were still alive. This is a good time to make yourself a chum bucket. Again, get a five-gallon bucket, remove the wire handle and replace it with a nylon rope. Next drill several one-quarter inch holes around the entire bucket for your chum to flow through. You don't need to drill any holes in the lid, but a few holes on the bottom won't hurt.

When was the last time that you changed your oil or lubed your engine? This too should be done every spring. If you have a trailerable boat, is the trailer in good condition for the upcoming season? Do you need to replace your brakes, tires, bearings or battery? You may want to think about renting a slip at a marina near your favorite fishing grounds especially in the spring or fall. Rent it by the month or by the week. It's very convenient to have your boat in the water and ready to go, if you would like to get in a couple hours of fishing. You won't have the hassle of unloading and loading your boat for each fishing trip.

How's your boat running? When is the last time you replaced your spark plugs, points, condenser or distributor cap? You want to be sure that when you turn the key in the morning that the engine will start and remain running the entire trip and throughout the season.

As you can see from this article, there are plenty of things that you can do to prepare for your fishing season this winter. Prepare yourself a check-list of the things you need to accomplish before that *"dreamed about opening day"* - you certainly don't want to be running to the tackle shop, store or parts dealer to pick up items. After all, the time spent accomplishing all the things that need attention, ultimately leads to one conclusion - *"less time on the water, perhaps . . , just perhaps . . . missing the catch of a life-time"*. So get ready now for the season, at least it's better than shoveling snow!

TROPHY STRIPED BASS - SPRING FISHING AT ITS BEST

Many of you will be pursuing that trophy striped bass this spring. You will have a small window of opportunity to capture one of these magnificent beauties. Striped bass, better known as rockfish in Maryland, come into the Chesapeake Bay and its tributaries to spawn every spring. Depending on the severity of the winter, stripers usually arrive in the bay in late February and over the next two months will proceed to their spawning grounds. Once they have spawned, usually by mid-May, most of them will begin to leave the bay and take part in the coastal migratory stock along the East Coast.

Maryland anglers have a golden opportunity during late April and May to capture a trophy rockfish. If you fish the middle or upper bay this may be your only chance to catch that BIG rockfish. With this in mind, I would like to share with you some of the techniques that I have learned over the past twenty years. These following techniques are the ones that many charterboat captains have developed and have been very productive over the years.

First let's talk about tackle. A nice quality rod of six to six and a half-feet, medium to medium-heavy action and either 20 to 40 lb. class test is what I would recommend, and a good quality reel such as a Penn 309 or 330GTI. Both of these reels are excellent pieces of equipment to use in the Bay and just as important is the fact that they are level wind reels. In my opinion, level wind reels are vitally important if you want to be an accomplished angler. The reason I say this is because you must know how much line you have let off your reel and where your lines are in the water column. Each time the level wind bar goes from one side plate to the other side plate you have let out approximately 10 feet of line. So if you have let out 140 feet off of your reel and you catch a fish with that rod you now have the capability to put that lure back into the same depth of water by letting out 140 feet. In turn, if you get another hit on that particular rod you may want to readjust your other lines either higher or deeper in the water column so as to fish near that same water depth.

Penn
Level-Wind
Reels

Line is another personal preference for each captain. Most charterboat captains use wire line, while the majority of recreational fishermen use monofilament. However, I prefer using a color-coded Dacron line with a lead core. This line comes in 25, 36 and 45 pound test, I prefer using the 36 pound test. This line does not stretch like mono and is a lot more forgiving than wire line. In addition, it is very beneficial if you are not using a level wind reel since it changes color every 10 yards. Thus giving you the ability to know how much line is off of your reels. I also have several reels loaded with the new synthetic line that has been developed in the past several years.

Our next topic would be lure selection. Remember that you always want to match the size of the lure with the size of the baitfish that the rockfish are feeding on. This time of the year large alewives are entering our bay to spawn. These adult alewives are 8 to 13 inches in length. The use of large spoons and bucktails best resemble the size of these baitfish. The two most popular spoons are #19 and #21 Tony Accettas and 9/0 and 11/0 Crippled Alewives. I prefer the Crippled Alewive lures over any other spoon because of their ability to be pulled through the water at a variety of trolling speeds, the lateral color line and the color of the lures themselves. Crippled Alewives also make a 13/0 spoon. Again this spoon comes in a variety of colors beside chrome and white. Don't be afraid to tie on a 13/0;

Match the size of the lure
with the size of the baitfish

remember the "*Big Bait - Big Fish*" theory. Because of their size most anglers are intimated when using them. Believe me, they really do work on catching that monster striper. Remember that we are fishing for a beast of 30 to 50 pounds. The following chart shows how I fish the variety of colored Crippled Alewives.

COLOR OF LURE IN RESPECT TO LIGHT AND DEPTH

Colors	Shallow	Mid-Depth	Deep
Red	▓		
Orange/Yellow	▓		
Pearl Dot		▓	
Green/Yellow		▓	▓
Blue/Purple		▓	▓
White	▓	▓	▓

When little light is entering the water, such as early morning, late evening or heavy overcast conditions, you should use chrome/white/gold lures. If good light is entering the water, such as partly cloudy days or bright sunny days, the use of fluorescent colors will be your best bet.

In addition to spoons, the traditional bucktail can still hold its own in catching fish. Use 8/0 to 10/0 bucktails to capture these trophy bass. Another excellent choice would be parachutes from 8 to 20 ounces. Both of these lures are widely used throughout the bay with white and chartreuse being the best choice of colors. Be sure that you add on attractors to help make their movement life-like while being trolled in the water. Generally 6 to 9 inch sassy shads or 8 inch twister tails are the correct size to use. Finally, the umbrella rig has really grown in popularity and has become one of the most used lures during the spring fishery. This rig is explained more fully in another article.

Leader line is very important! At some point this is the only thing between you and the fish. Do yourself a favor and purchase good quality leader line material. Don't be *"penny-wise and dollar foolish"* at this point. Buy a 1/4 pound spool of Ande, Trilene, Stren or any other major brand line. You will probably spend $6 to $9 for a 1/4 pound spool that will last for years instead of paying $1.59 for a cheaper brand that you cannot depend on. I highly recommend using 60 pound test mono-filament leader line material. Heavy leader line is needed because of the great amount of stress that is caused by catching a large rockfish during the spring season. I make my leader lines 36 feet in length. I also use ball bearing swivels in order to take out all of the twist that is put into your leader-line by using large spoons. Once again, these swivels are much

Ball Bearing
Swivel with
Coast Lock

more expensive than regular swivels, but they are well worth your investment. Refer to the illustration, located on page 16, of my trolling rig that I use while fishing for stripers in the spring-time.

You will notice that I am using a double rig, I have now just improved my chances of catching that rockfish by 100%. Double rigging all of my lines, allows me to pull an average of 24 to 28

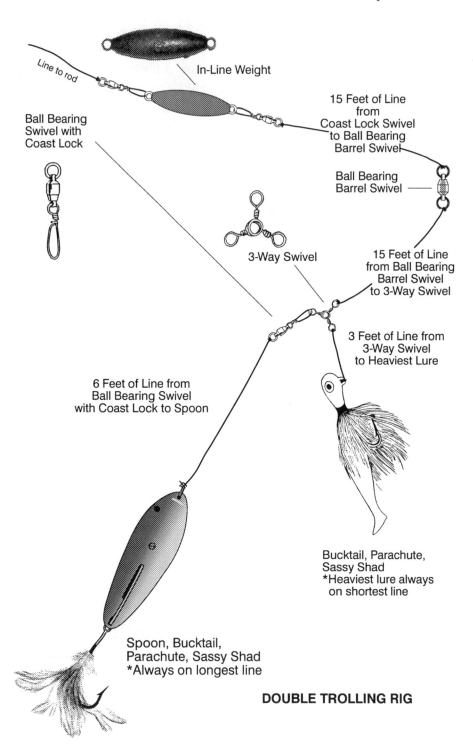

Line to rod

In-Line Weight

15 Feet of Line
from
Coast Lock Swivel
to Ball Bearing
Barrel Swivel

Ball Bearing
Swivel with
Coast Lock

Ball Bearing
Barrel Swivel

3-Way Swivel

15 Feet of Line
from Ball Bearing
Barrel Swivel
to 3-Way Swivel

3 Feet of Line from
3-Way Swivel
to Heaviest Lure

6 Feet of Line from
Ball Bearing Swivel
with Coast Lock to Spoon

Bucktail, Parachute,
Sassy Shad
*Heaviest lure always
on shortest line

Spoon, Bucktail,
Parachute, Sassy Shad
*Always on longest line

DOUBLE TROLLING RIG

baits behind my boat. Now you can see how important it is to know how much line is off your reels and how deep your lures are in the water.

Speed is one of the most important aspects of trolling. Select the rod that has a large spoon as your lure and let out your leader line to the snap swivel or sinker. I would recommend a #21 Tony to be used here. Observe your lure in the water to see if it is working properly. Either speed up or slow down your boat and watch which speed works your spoon the best. Now let out your line to the desired length while going in the same direction. After setting the drag and placing your rod in the rod holder - STOP - and observe what your rod tip is doing. The action of this lure really works the rod tip and is much more pronounced then using a Crippled Alewive. This is going to be your speed indicator for the remainder of the day. The tip of your rod will be dipping, bobbing or weaving ever so often to show that your lure is working properly. Due to tide, wind, and change of direction during the course of a day, your boat speed will change, thus changing the motion of your lures. Watch your rod tip and achieve that same motion as when you originally put your line overboard throughout the entire day to know that your spoon is working properly.

Illustrated below is my recommendation for setting your trolling lines in the spring. By using this set of lengths and weights, it should allow you to be at the correct depth to catch that trophy striper. In addition, it will allow you to troll all day without getting your lines tangled. Remember to make wide enough turns to also help maintain untangled lines.

SETTING TROLLING LINES

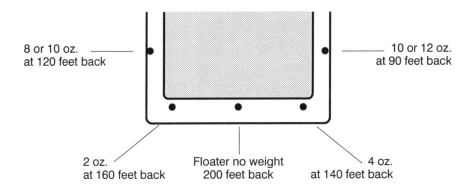

8 or 10 oz. at 120 feet back

10 or 12 oz. at 90 feet back

2 oz. at 160 feet back

Floater no weight 200 feet back

4 oz. at 140 feet back

Finally, I would like to suggest a trolling pattern that should enable you to have an opportunity to capture a trophy bass. I prefer trolling cross-tide or an east-west pattern. Trolling diagonally from east-west or vice versa, will allow you to have a window of opportunity to be in the correct water depth that the stripers are using while exiting the bay. Rockfish like to follow the bay's channel edges down the bay. If the fish are following the western edge of the channel in 70 feet of water down the bay, due to tide, current, etc. and you are trolling a north-south pattern in 50 feet of water on the eastern edge, you will never have a hook-up. But if you troll east to west, your lures at some point in time will be in that 70 feet of water. Remember the bay is cool and will warm only through warm days and sunlight. I fish all of my lures within the first 25 feet of the surface, regardless of whether I am trolling in 50 feet water or 120 feet.

Larry Siperek of Pennsylvania
displaying a trophy bass of 36 inches, caught while trolling in the spring
outside Chesapeake Beach

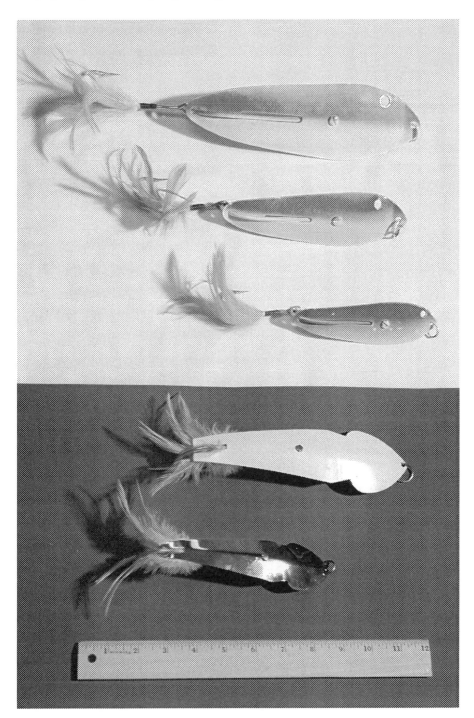

Spring Spoons

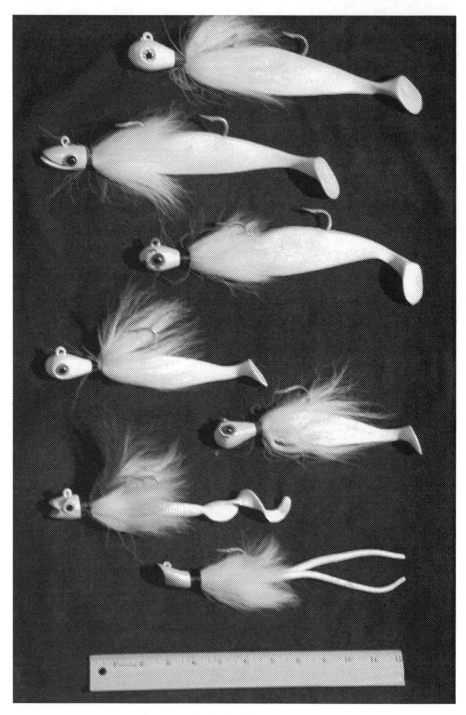

Spring Bucktails

Spring Parachutes

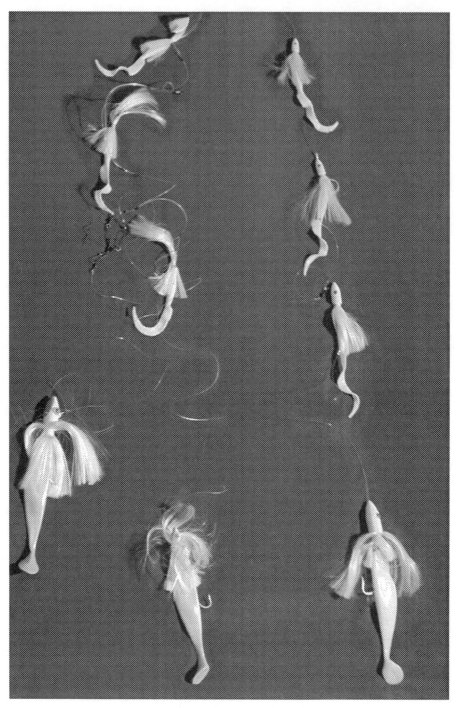

Spring Daisy Chains

Bill Windley holding his rockfish caught during the 2003 trophy season

"Big Bait - Big Fish"

Blaine Kurrle with a 39 inch striper caught during the spring of 2001

UMBRELLA RIGS FOR SPRING STRIPERS

Several years ago the Chesapeake Bay fishing community was introduced to a real radical looking fishing lure. This lure looked so complicated that you knew that it had to get tangled before you could catch a fish on it.

I first saw this lure in action while I was acting captain of "*Spoons*", a 36-foot Jersey that belonged to Fred Meers, who at the time was the owner of Crippled Alewive Lures. Several MSSA members were on-board that chilly November day in '92.

Little did I know at that time, the umbrella rig would be the hottest lure to hit the Chesapeake Bay in decades. The umbrella rig has gained its place in every sportfishermen's list of proven baits for the Bay. This lure has been used for many years by anglers in several states to our north for bluefish. When the umbrella rig was brought to Maryland, it had a surgical hose or bucktail as bait with 8 to 12 smaller tube hoses as an attractor. Unfortunately, these smaller attractor hoses had hooks on each hose making it illegal to fish in Maryland waters. Maryland laws state that you are only allowed two hooks per line. Due to the law in Maryland, umbrella rigs are rigged with plain sassy shads, twister tails or hoses with no hooks as attractors.

Umbrella rigs are available at many of the major tackle shops or boating supply stores. You can get them already rigged but they often have too many hooks if they come prepackaged to the store. I've found it best to buy the bare rig and outfit it with your own lures. They are easy to rig and you can use your own imagination on how they should be rigged. Generally, we use large sassy shads as attractors on each arm. You can attach these shads by snap swivels to each part of the arm and run an 18 to 20 inch leader from the center point for your main line. You can either use a bucktail, parachute or a large spoon as your bait. However, if you use a Crippled Alewive or Tony as your bait, you should use a ball bearing swivel at the end of your leader line and attach it to the middle of the rig. Many captains use double rigs or baits on their umbrella rigs. This can be accomplished by using one arm of the rig and attaching your lures on each end of the wire by an 18 inch leader line. Either use the same size bucktails or parachutes as your lures.

Umbrella
Rig

I like to use 6 inch shads and attach them to the swivel by opening the swivel and using the wire portion just like a hook. Thread the wire into the shad and then back out of its back leaving enough wire exposed to re-snap the swivel. I also like to use the same color combination throughout the rig. If I'm going to use all chartreuse shads, I like to use a green and yellow Crippled Alewive or a chartreuse parachute or bucktail.

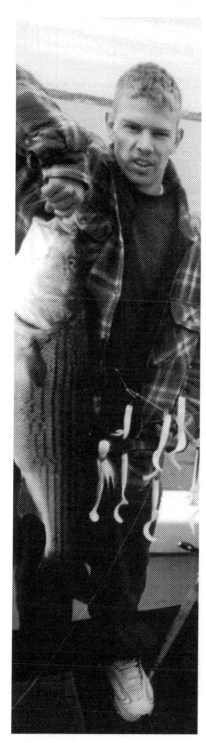

Umbrella rigs come in many sizes. They come in eight-arm rigs down to four-arms. You can purchase a four-arm rig that measures 12 inches across or one that measures 19 inches. Then you have one which has six-arms and measures 13 inches across. Remember the larger the rig and number of attractors create more drag when you bring in that line.

These rigs are very hard to fish and retrieve due to the tremendous amount of drag they create while pulling them through the water. I would suggest that you use a 3/0 or better yet a 4/0 class rod to fish these rigs. Although they can be fished with wire line with no weights, I would recommend adding 6 to 8 ounces of weight and fishing them back 100 feet or more. Another little secret that I would like to pass on is how to place them in the water. Hold the entire rig horizontally above the water and drop it in and feed out the leader line as quickly as possible. DO NOT leader the line out slowly, as this may cause the rig to come to the surface, twist and become tangled.

The easiest way to store or carry your umbrella rigs on and off the boat is to place them in a 16-inch pizza box. If you have several rigs, you may want to purchase an umbrella rig carrying case which cost around $20.

Try fishing an umbrella rig this spring season, especially during the MSSA Spring Tournament. It's a "*Hot Lick*".

 # NUMBERING YOUR RODS

If you are straight trolling (not bottom bouncing) with multiple rods, it is advisable to number your rods to their positions on the boat.

As the drawing on the proceeding page illustrates, I have designated a number for each of my rod holders on my boat. Since you may have rods and reels that look very similar, you may want each rod to stay in a particular location due to the length of line, sinker weight or lure on that rod.

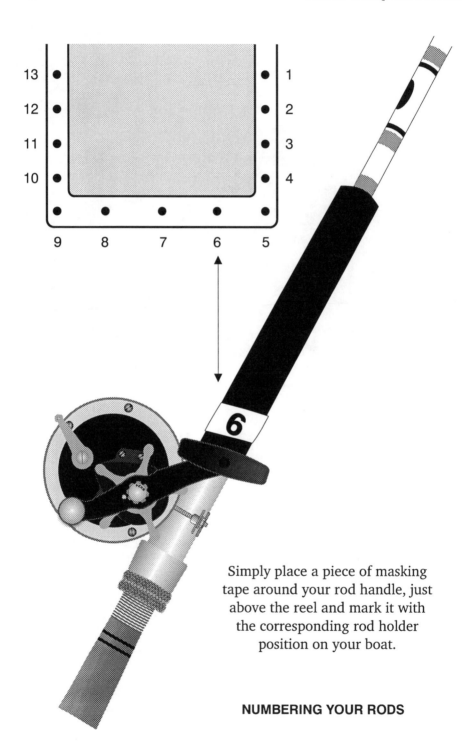

Simply place a piece of masking tape around your rod handle, just above the reel and mark it with the corresponding rod holder position on your boat.

NUMBERING YOUR RODS

 # HOW TO RIG A STINGER HOOK

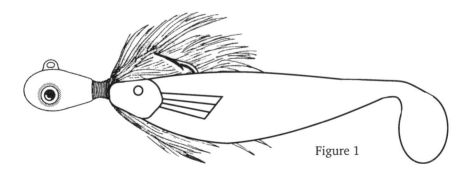

Figure 1

1. Take your sassy shad and place it up against your bucktail to see where the hook of the lure will protrude through the back of the shad.

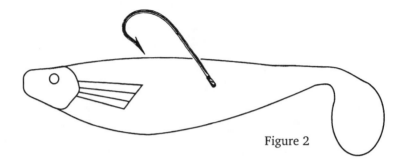

Figure 2

2. Take your stinger hook and puncture the spot on the shad where the lure hook will come out of the shad.

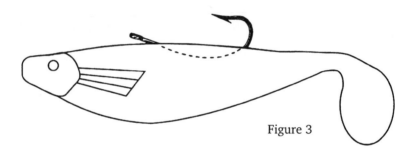

Figure 3

3. Push the hook into the shad up to the curvature of the hook. Leave the eye of the hook exposed.

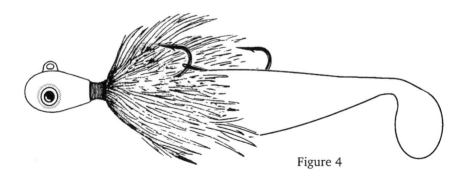

Figure 4

4. Take your bucktail and insert its hook out of the back of the shad into your stinger hook eye.

 # PLANER BOARDS

If you have spent any time fishing the Chesapeake Bay in the last couple of years, you have seen quite a number of boats pulling planer boards. They are becoming increasingly popular each year. The reason is simple, they catch fish! They move your lines away from the boat to capture those fish that might have been spooked by your boat or motor. It also gives you the ability to cover much more area while trolling. If you attach a 100 foot line on each planer board, you are now covering approximately 150 to 170 feet of water behind and to the sides of your boat. If you are not using these boards, you are only covering, at best, up to 20 feet directly behind your boat.

Planer boards are an excellent way to find fish. The reason they are so effective is your ability to cover much more territory. In addition, fish will spook because of engine noise or because of an on-coming boat. Fish have a tendency to move off to the side of a boat that is trolling. Now they will swim right into the path of your lines off of your planer board.

To purchase or make the size of your planer board depends on the size of your boat. Large boats, such as charter  boats, may have a set of boards that are five feet long and three feet wide. These are usually way too large to have enough room to store on your boat. However, a set of planer boards of eight inches by twenty-eight inches should be small enough for you to handle.

Your boards will be angled on the front to make it travel to starboard or port. Place a strong line or even a heavy weed whacker line to your boards. A 100 foot line should be all you need for each board. Attach a hook or "C" clasp line to one end in order to attach it to your boat while in use. Tie the other end directly to your board.

At the start of your fishing day, place each board overboard and attach one end to the highest part of your boat as possible. After they are in position let out your first line to the desired length and engage the reel. Next, attach a rubber band on your line near your rod tip. A simple loop knot will do. Now attach the rubber band to a shower curtain hook. When I first started, I used wire shower curtain hooks; however, I switched to round plastic ones, usually white in color in order to see them better. Since that time, I am now using aluminum clips (mountain climbing clips type) in various colors. I switched to these because they are much easier to use hooking up to your planer board line and they are very visible. After you have attached the hooks to your planer line, disengage the reel; allow the hook to travel down the line until you feel that your line is far enough away from the boat. Lock up your reel and set the drag before putting it into your rod holder. You

can fish two to five lines off of each planer board. Just set them approximately 20 to 25 feet apart on the line. When a fish strikes, it will snap the rubber band and the fight is on.

After catching the fish, play out the other lines on the board until your lures are set in the proper position. Let out your line that you just reeled in, as this will now become your closest line to the boat. Just keep the rotation up throughout the day and at the end of the day, when you pull your planer boards in, just remove the shower curtain hooks at that time. You may want to carry a couple dozen or so shower hooks. Place your engine in neutral, to make it an easy task in retrieving your planer board.

The illustration on page 40 demonstrates that the boards are behind and to the sides. I have placed an X as to your position on the line. Remember, if you put out 150 feet off of your reel and attach it to the planer line and then you let your line out 60 to 100 feet on the planer line, you could end up bringing that fish in on 250 feet of line. You may be better off if you only let out 50 to 60 feet off of your reel and run it down the planer line 50 to 80 feet. In this illustration, I have drawn my five stern rod positions and lines and how I have set up my four rods to each of my planer boards, creating an open lane in order to bring the fish to the boat.

Always let out your furthest line from the boat first. This rod should go to your rod holder closest to the bow of the boat. Each rod should be placed in order as you let out your line down the planer board line. Your last line should be the shortest and placed toward the stern of the boat, as illustrated.

Depending on how many rods you want to fish could answer how many lines you want to use on your planer boards. I would suggest only attaching two lines on each board until you become more familiar in using your planer boards.

HOW TO BUILD PLANER BOARDS

A set of planer boards can cost you up to 100 bucks if purchased from a retail store. Why not build your own and use the money you save to buy more fishing tackle?

<u>Materials List for Building Two Planer Boards:</u>

(4)	1" or 1-1/4" x 8" x 28" pieces of redwood
(6)	12" x 5/16" threaded rods
(2)	6" x 5/16" eyebolts
(28)	5/16" washers
(28)	5/16" nuts
(1 qt.)	quality wood sealant
(1 qt.)	high-visibility or orange paint
(150 ft.)	planer board line, something low stretch and small in diameter, like a nylon

<u>Tools Required</u>:
Hand, radial or table saw, a miter saw, plane or rasp, tape measure and a 5/16" combination or adjustable wrench

PLANER BOARD TIP

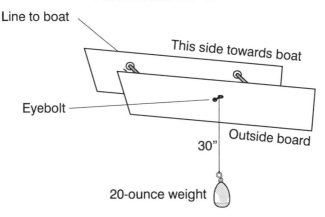

Line to boat

This side towards boat

Eyebolt

Outside board

30"

20-ounce weight

After you have come accustomed to using your planer board, you will want to fish additional lines. Another tip that I would like to pass on is to tie a line approximately 30 inches in length and place it on the outside board. Tie on a 20 ounce weight in order to keep the board running smoothly through the water, especially on those rough days.

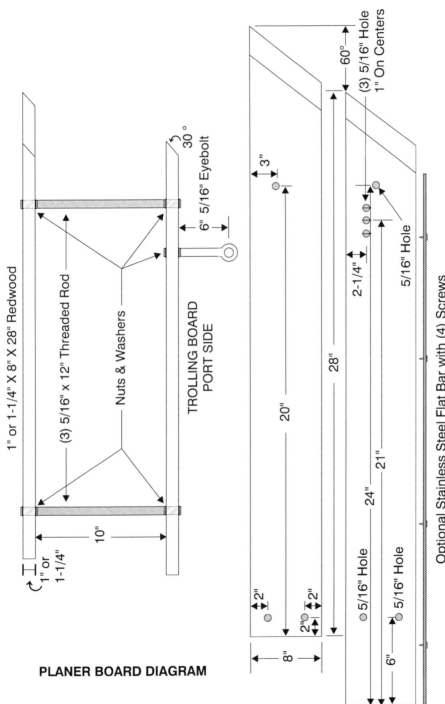

PLANER BOARD DIAGRAM

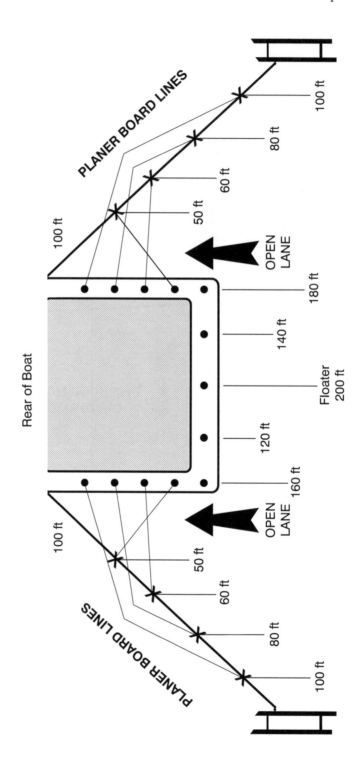

"Woody" showing off his trophy

HOW TO MAKE A DUMMY LINE

You will need the following material:

- 25 Feet of 1/8 or 1/4 inch nylon line
- 12 Feet of 150 pound test monofilament
- One 5 pound weight and one 16 ounce weight (cigar shaped)
- Three 300 pound snap swivels
- One 24 to 32 inch bungee cord

To start, put a snap swivel on one end of your nylon line. Attach it to the five pound weight. Make a loop in the other end and this attaches to your stern boat cleat. From this loop, come down approximately six to eight inches or as long as the main line is away from the transom. Put in another loop knot and attach one end of the bungee cord. Here is where it gets a little tricky! You will have to play with the line until you can form a loop in your line while forming the other loop that will hold your bungee cord. The loop should be made in your line in order to have approximately four inches between your bungee cord and your main line. This will have to be done while you are on the water and trolling. If you hold both ends of your main line and pull, the bungee cord should come even with your main line (see example). This is how you can tell when you have a fish on your line. The bungee and the main line will pull even with each other.

Next, tie on your remaining swivels to each end of your monofilament line. One end will attach to the five pound weight, while the other end will attach to the 16 ounce weight.

Bungee Cord
&
Snap Swivel

The reason you should add the additional small weight is to keep your line out of all of the turbulence created by the five pound weight. By adding the additional line and weight, it will drop your line and lure below the turbulence.

Depending on the time of year and the size of fish I am targeting, I use anywhere from a 30 to 100 pound test leader line. In the spring when I am targeting large rockfish or bluefish, I use a 100 pound test leader. Unlike fishing with a rod and reel that has a drag system on the reel, there is nothing to offset the stress when a fish is on the line. This is a straight pull with no give in the line.

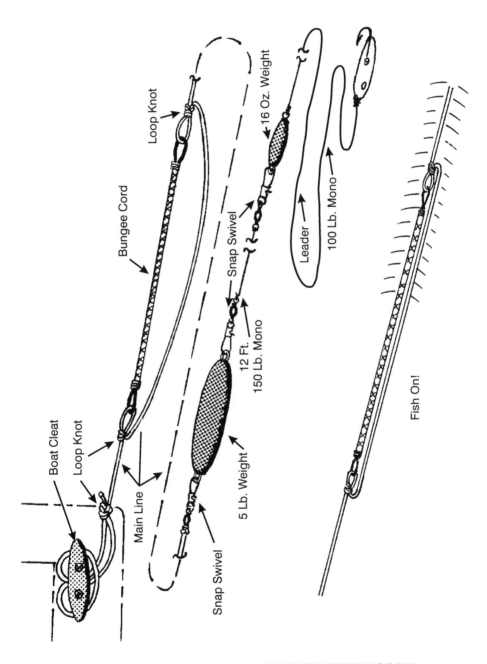

DUMMY LINE DIAGRAM

HOW DEEP ARE YOUR LURES?

*Credit - This article written by George Pieper of Annapolis
and printed by permission*

The development in the last few years of very strong, very thin, and essentially non-stretching fishing lines provides fishermen with new alternatives to the monofilament, wire, and lead-core trolling lines that we used in the past. The new lines have great advantages. They are extremely sensitive because they don't stretch the way monofilament does, and they don't kink and sometimes break the way wire does. And, in addition to being tough and abrasion resistant, they are very thin, which means they are subject to less drag and can take lures to a greater depth with less weight.

I became interested in the question of how deep trolling lures run when they are pulled behind a fishing boat, and how I ran a number of lures at different speeds in a tow tank in the hydrodynamics laboratory of the U. S. Naval Academy in Annapolis and measured the drag and lift forces exerted by the lures as they were pulled through the water. Starting with these forces, I then applied the laws of fluid dynamics to the leader, in-line sinker, and main line to write a computer program that can calculate how deep each of these lures would run.

The New Lines

The main lines for which results were obtained in 1993 were 40 lb. test monofilament, 0.020 inch diameter wire, and a 35 lb. test lead core. Now through the courtesy of their manufacturers and engineering representatives, I have gotten the necessary constants (line diameter and linear density) to apply the program to a number of the new lines: 35 lb. test Spectron, 30 and 50 lb. test FireLine, and 30, 40, 50, and 60 lb. test Spider Wire main lines. At the request of a friend who uses it, I have also included a 30 lb. test Dacron line.

The program now is the same as before in that it still uses a Tony 21, 19, or 18 spoon, a Crippled Alewive 11/0, 9/0, or 7/0, or a surgical hose lure, attached to a 30 foot, 40 lb. test monofilament leader, an in-line sinker, and a main line. It is able now to select from one or more of eleven different lines, seven different lures, an in-line sinker of adjustable weight, and any desired boat speed and main line length. In fact, the only thing not currently adjustable is the 30 ft. 40 lb. test mono leader and that could be changed, too, if necessary.

With such flexibility in the program, it's easy to get swamped with results. It turns out that the same approaches to using the data that I developed in 1993 are still valid: To take account of boat speed, for all lines, sinker depth at 2.5 mph is 1.3 times that at 3 mph, and at 3.5 mph it is 0.8 times that at 3 mph. Heavy lures like a Tony 21 or Crippled Alewive 11/0 will run about three feet below the sinker depth while a light bucktail or surgical hose will be only about one foot deeper.

It's also true that the accurate linear relationships between sinker depth and sinker weight for line lengths between 50 and 200 ft. that I found for the monofilament and wire lines worked with earlier, also apply individually to all the new lines. So it is possible to simply extend the trolling depths chart from the 1993 article to the new lines to again answer the question: *"If there are fish at some depth on the meter, what combination of line length and sinker weight should I use to get to that depth?"* Results are given in the Trolling Lure Depth Table for 40 lb. test monofilament, 0.020 inch diameter wire, 30 lb. test Dacron, 35 lb. test lead core, 35 lb. test Spectron, 30 and 50 lb. test FireLine, and 30, 40, 50, and 60 lb. test Spider Wire main lines. Line diameters, either measured or obtained from the manufacturers are also given for each line type.

Trolling Lure Depth Table

The Trolling Lure Depth Table tells what combinations of line length and sinker weight to use to reach the desired depth for a series of depths at 5-foot intervals. Main line length is measured from the sinker to where the line breaks the water's surface behind the boat. A boat speed of 3 mph is assumed, and a standard 2 ft. of depth is taken for leader and lure, to be adjusted for the kind of lure. The resultant sinker weights are rounded off to the nearest ounce.

Some observations:

1. The Spider Wires, being the thinnest, get deeper with less sinker weight than the other lines. The Spider Wires are also very close to each other in the weight needed to achieve a given depth as the line strength is changed by 10 lb. increments. There would not seem to be much point in using more than one strength of Spider Wire for a number of trolling rods.

2. The FireLines behave similarly to the Spider Wires, but require a few (usually three to five) more ounces of sinker weight to reach the same depth. 35 lb. test Spectron is very close to 30 lb. test FireLine, usually within one ounce.

3. All the new lines are qualitatively different from the lead core and wire lines, and good old

monofilament is in a class by itself because it's so lightweight and has comparatively such a large diameter. It takes a lot of weight to get it down with the others, on the other hand, it's the only one that can keep your lures at ten feet or less with more than 50 feet of line out, unless you go to zero sinker weight. The depth achieved depends much more strongly on the lure type than it does with a sinker weight greater than zero.

How Your Line Looks Under Water

Figure 1, located on page 49, shows the computed shapes of lines in the water for a boat moving from left to right across the page for several main line lengths of up to 200 ft. and one particular combination of lure and sinker. (Think of your boat moving to the right and located where the name of a line is, or at some other point along that curve for a shorter line.) The 30 ft. mono leader is also shown. Note that for line lengths up to about 120 feet, 35 lb. test Spectron, 30 lb. test FireLine and .020" wire are very nearly indistinguishable.

Some Lure Depths for Trolling

Figure 2, located on page 50, shows an arrangement of five lines off the stern of a trolling boat going three mph. It was originally put together to show how to get to a spread in depths of 5 to 25 feet while searching for fish, using monofilament and wire lines. Now added are the depths to which the previously chosen combinations of sinker weight and line length would get if the lines are of 35 lb. test Spectron and 30 lb. test Spider Wire. The other possible wires can be related to these using the main chart.

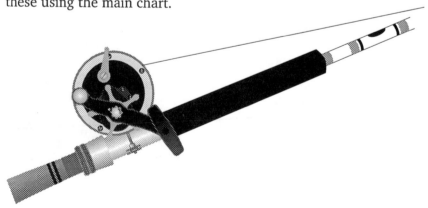

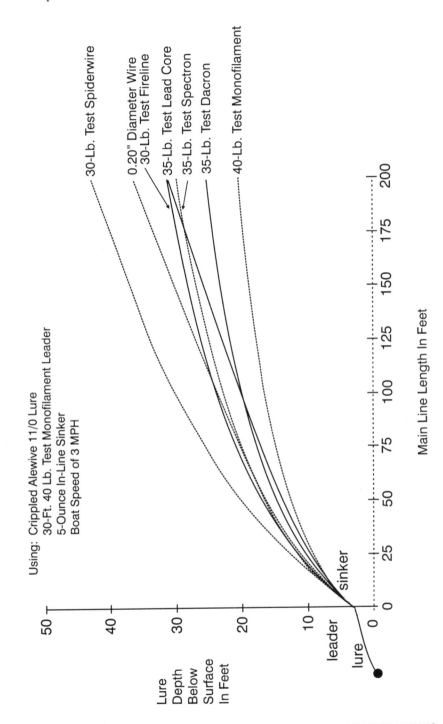

FIGURE 1 - LURE DEPTH VS. MAIN LINE LENGTH FOR SEVEN MAIN LINES

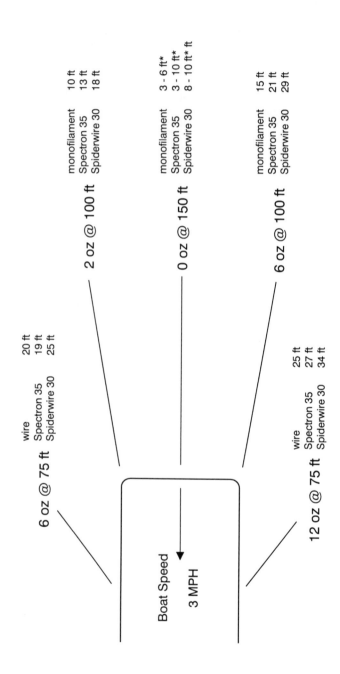

FIGURE 2 - LURE DEPTH FOR TROLLING

 # WRAPPING UP YOUR LINES

Whenever I am through for the day of trolling, I like to stow my rods with leader line and lures still intact. This can be done simply by the use of rubber bands or bungee cords. I first started using rubber bands to secure my lures on my rod. I found two problems with using them. First and most obvious is that they have a tendency to break easily. Secondly, after a while they melt onto your rod and become very difficult to remove. Hank Devito, Captain of the "*Afternoon Delight*" gave a demonstration at one of the local MSSA chapter meetings. He was using six-inch bungee cords to secure his lures rather than rubber bands. Since that time I have switched to using bungee cords. They work great. *Thanks, Hank!*

1. First, wind in your line until the swivel from your main line is close to the rod tip and remove your sinker. Grab your leader line and wrap it around the opposite side of the handle on your reel. When you get within three feet of your lure, wrap your leader line, or three-way swivel around your reel. If you are using a tandem rig, bring your lure up from the reel toward the rod tip.

2. Next, take your bungee cord and hook one end on your lure and stretch the other end to a rod guide. Don't stretch your bungee cord out tight. Just make it tight enough to hold your lure in place.

The next time you want to go fishing, all you have to do is to take off the bungee cords, unwrap your leader line and drop your lures in the water and you are fishing. There's no hassle about making up leader lines or tying on lures. You're ready to start fishing as soon as you slow the boat down to trolling speed.

 # EEL FISHING FOR ROCKFISH

Eel fishing for rockfish is one of the most exciting ways to catch these beautiful creatures. By mid-October the Bay waters should start to cool, thus causing the stripers to school and feed aggressively for the winter. We are allowed to keep two fish per day with a minimum length of 18 inches. However, only one of your daily creel of rockfish can measure over 28 inches. In other words, you can keep two rockfish of 20 inches in length but not two rockfish of 30 inches. The major issue with fishing with eels or live bait is that often you cannot set the hook quick enough before the rockfish swallows the bait. Keep this in mind if you are eel fishing and you have already caught and kept your rockfish. If you lip hook your fish, you may want to release him in order to continue to fish. If you have caught your limit, I would like to highly recommend that you stop fishing with eels or live bait. If you still would like to continue fishing, I suggest that you use artificial baits such as bucktails in order to reduce fishing mortality. Remember to handle the fish as gently as possible and try to leave the fish in the water whenever possible. Try to use a de-hooker, since this will allow you to release the fish without touching it and removing the protective film or slime.

I would like to recommend a 6 to 6-1/2 foot medium-action rod and reel filled with 12 to 17 pound test line. I like to snell on a 4/0 or 6/0 hook on a 30 inch leader line of 50 to 60 pound test. The reason to use a heavy leader line is due to very rough (shell and oyster bars) structures you may fishing over which can be very abrasive to your line. Another reason is, if the rockfish is deep hooked in the mouth, the inside of his lips are almost like sandpaper which could also abuse your line. On the other end of my leader line, I tie on a snap swivel that will be attached to a cigar shaped sinker. Using a snap swivel at the end of your running line from your reel, will allow you to change weights during the course of the day depending on the tide. Try to use only enough weight to keep your eel on the bottom, usually a 1 to 2 ounce sinker is enough. Either use a bell shaped sinker or a cigar shaped sinker; I prefer the cigar shaped sinker.

One helpful hint is to ice down your eels when you leave the dock. By the time you get to your fishing area, the eels are lethargic and are much easier to handle. Use a dry rag or paper towel to hold your eels while placing it on your hook. As soon as the eel is dropped into the warmer water, it will come back to life. I prefer hooking the eel through his bottom lip to top lip, unless I am fishing heavy structures such as bridges or wrecks, in which case I hook them from eye to eye. A good depth finder is essential when eel fishing for rockfish. Once you have located the fish

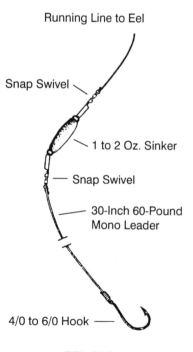

Running Line to Eel

Snap Swivel

1 to 2 Oz. Sinker

Snap Swivel

30-Inch 60-Pound Mono Leader

4/0 to 6/0 Hook

EEL RIG

on your depth finder, drop a marker where the fish are located. Position your boat up tide to drift directly back toward your marker. Once you are over the fish, drop your line straight down. Do not cast your line away from the boat; the fish are directly underneath you at this point. When you feel a *"pick up"*, let the fish have a chance to get the lip hooked eel into his mouth before setting the hook. Often you will feel a couple of tugs and then the line will start to run off in a straight direction. Now is the time to set the hook!

I would like to suggest that you net these fish, since they will be well over the 18 inch minimum size. The average length of fish that I caught in the fall while eel fishing was 25 inches, with quite a few going over 36 inches. Trying to bring this size fish out of the water with your rod and reel will result in your line breaking.

The major problem with eel fishing is that you always draw a crowd. The second year was no different from the first year of rockfishing with eels. It is almost like *"bumper cars"* but on the water. Remember to be courteous and wait your turn to fall into line to make your drift. After you have made your drift *"over the spot"* and if you were lucky enough to have caught a fish, take your time and proceed slowly back to the head of the pack to make another drift. Too many inconsiderate anglers (several other names could apply) were afraid that the fish would move off the spot and ran full throttle back to the front of the pack. This caused several boats to be bumped - due to their boat wake. Don't get caught up into this frenzy! It is better to find another school of fish - than to have your boat damaged.

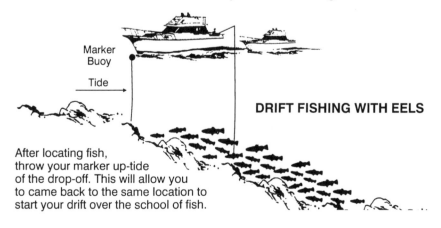

Marker Buoy

Tide

DRIFT FISHING WITH EELS

After locating fish, throw your marker up-tide of the drop-off. This will allow you to came back to the same location to start your drift over the school of fish.

Not hard finding the rockfish, but tough to find a place to drop your line! Wall to wall boats drift fishing at one of the favorite *Parking Lots* in the Upper Bay

 # EELING MADE EASY ROCKFISH

Illustrated on the following page is a convenient and easy way to construct a live eel bait bucket. I have cut another five gallon bucket approximately 3 inches from the bottom and inserted it into my first bucket. Drill a number of holes in the bottom of the inserted bucket, so that the melted ice will drip through the holes. The reason for installing the inverted bucket, is to elevate the eels, and to keep them from drowning in the melted ice.

Place your eels in the bucket and then fill the bucket with crushed ice. By the time you reach your fishing grounds, the eels should be lethargic and much easier to handle.

Remember - you must still use a DRY rag or paper towels to hold the eel while placing the them on your hook. Your eels will stay alive all day in the ice and you will not have to worry about losing them out of an overboard bait container.

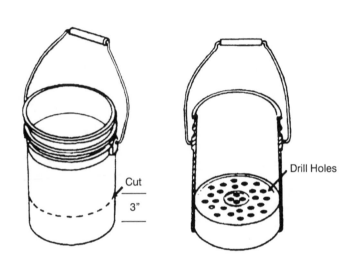

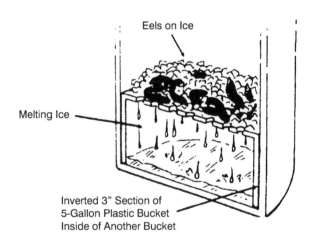

LIVE EEL BUCKET DIAGRAM

1. Through bottom lip and upper lip.

2. Through bottom lip and out of eye.

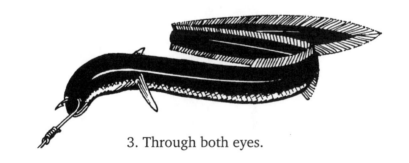

3. Through both eyes.

4. Through the mouth and out of lower lip.

FOUR WAYS TO HOOK A LIVE EEL

My Uncle Richard with a nice Father's Day striper caught while chumming near the Green Flasher below Thomas Point Light

 # CHUMMING FOR ROCKFISH

Chumming has become the more popular fishing method for catching striped bass in the last few years during the summer. Spring will find more anglers trolling due to the fish not being schooled at that time of year. Most rockfish are still in the tributaries participating in their primeval spawning rituals. Maryland regulations do not allow fishing in these river systems until the 1st of June. Fishermen are fishing primarily on the migratory stock that inhabit the East Coast throughout the remainder of the year. During the spring, anglers can cover more ground by trolling, since most of the stripers are individual fish who are leaving the Bay and are heading toward their summer quarters off of New England.

In addition, the Bay's water temperature is still cool, hovering around 60 degrees in the spring, late April through May. As the water warms, stripers will make their way out of the tributaries to their summer haunts in the Bay.

Chumming is a fairly simple way to catch fish. The concept behind chumming is that you make the fish come to you rather than you riding around the Bay looking for the fish. Chumming is an easy method for even the novice to be successful. Don't just go to an area and drop your anchor. Before anchoring, search the area to see if you can find the fish on your depth finder and anchor up-tide of the fish.

There are several "*schools of thought*" on exactly how to chum for rockfish. For the first method, you need to get a five gallon bucket and drill several 1/4 inch holes through the top, bottom and sides of the bucket. Remove the wire handle and replace with nylon line. This line should be long enough to go around the bucket and have a couple of feet left to tie off of your rear boat cleat. Now, place your frozen chum that you just purchased from the tackle shop into your five gallon bucket. You are ready to begin chumming. Please remember that the amount of chum exiting the bucket will depend upon how much of the bucket is in the water. This flow must be controlled by rising or lowering your chum bucket in the water. Some of the variables to remember are wave action, tidal flow, current and boat or ship wakes. All of these can force too much chum to escape your bucket prematurely. You should have a light and steady flow from your bucket but not so much as to feed the fish. You are looking for a few particles at a time. You should try to keep a steady, even flow of chum coming out of your bucket. Most of the chum that you buy locally is ground up alewives.

Another more controlled way to chum is to ladle it over the side of your boat by means of a cup, spoon or ladle. Place your chum into a bucket and add bay water, as you scoop your chum and throw it over the side of your boat, it will contain particles and the smell of your chum. You must continue to ladle this chum constantly over the side every minute or so. This will create a "*chum slick*" behind your boat. This slick is merely your chum being carried off by the tide. Fish will be attracted down tide and will begin to move up your chum line. This is why it is so important to always keep your chum line going. This will allow you to "*hold*" the fish directly behind your boat.

Create a "*Chum Slick*"
Behind Your Boat

Another simple way to chum is to grind your alewives on the boat. You will need a large meat grinder, either electric or manual. Position the grinder on the side of the boat on a board and place your alewives into the grinder. As the alewives are ground onto the board, simply flick the ground-up meat overboard every so often.

Next, after you have established a flow of chum behind your boat, you will notice a slick on the water surface. The oil in the ground up fish creates this slick. Spinning rods and reels should be used in the medium action range, from six to six and a half feet. Tie a snap swivel to the end of your running line. Next, tie on a 30 to 36 inch leader line and your hook. I strongly urge you to use circle hooks instead of the traditional "J" hooks. Circle hooks are designed to hook a fish in his mouth while "J" hooks have a tendency to gut hook a fish if you wait too long to set the hook. In fact, you will probably have more "*hook-ups*" using circle hooks because you allow the fish to hook themselves. They are designed to allow the fish to swallow the hook. As the fish moves off, it will pull back out of their stomachs or throats due to it being round. Yet as it starts to exit their mouth, the hook will rotate and catch and lodge in their jaw. Be sure to check your bait periodically. If the "*bite*" is on and your rod is not getting a strike, you're probably out of bait on your hook.

Bait can be frozen alewives, fresh fish, live spot or white perch. Cut your alewives into one-inch strips starting right behind the head and work back to the tail. A serrated knife works best as you must cut through the fish; sometimes these alewives may still be frozen. If you are only catching sub-legal rockfish in the area, you may want to cut the bait length-wise first and cut smaller pieces of bait from that fillet in order to target a smaller grade of fish that is of legal size. You may also want to try live lining as you are chumming. Live lining is catching small fish, such as spot or white perch while fishing and placing the entire live fish on the hook. Drop the line behind the boat, leaving out enough line for the fish to reach the bottom. You will know when a rockfish picks up your baitfish and moves off. The rod will be bent in half and stay bent, especially if you are using circle hooks.

Last, but not least, is tide. Tide is very important when chumming. Tide carries your chum either up or down the Bay to attract fish to feed in your chum line. Remember you are anchored and you're trying to attract fish to come to you rather than trolling where you must find the fish. The best time to chum is the first two hours of a rising tide or the last two hours of a falling tide. You can also fish on a slack tide if you have had a well established chum line before the tide has stopped. Of course, you won't be as busy as on a moving tide, but still continue to chum during this period as well. You may want to add some weight while chumming. Try floating a line or two with no weight and a couple of lines with a half ounce or more. Once the tide gets off, you may have to add additional weight, even up to three ounces in order to get it down to the fish.

Remember to handle these stripers carefully. If it is a sub-legal fish, try to get the fish back into the water just as quickly as possible. Try not to touch them as you remove the hook. Try using one of the many hook-outs that are on the market today. By removing the hook, the survival rate increases dramatically. Handle the fish as little as possible in order to keep from removing the protective slime or film that fights off harmful diseases.

Ed Kurcharski displaying a nice pair of stripers after a chumming trip
onboard the *"Oh Thank Heaven"*

Frank Holden holding a 30 inch plus rockfish caught
chumming off of Thomas Point

Laura Leech of the Atlantic States Marine Fishery Commission showing off her
1st rockfish caught in the Chesapeake Bay

 # CIRCLE HOOKS

For the past several years I have been promoting the use of circle
hooks while chumming for rockfish in the Chesapeake Bay. Circle
hooks are the way to go to help preserve our fishery. Several fishing
associations, and the DNR have worked very hard together to bring
this fishery back to a restored status. There is no reason to blatantly
abuse this resource.

I would like to encourage anglers fishing for rockfish to use circle
hooks. Due to the design of circle hooks, they will generally lip-hook a
rockfish if fished properly. Be sure that you use a non-offset circle
hook. To this point, in a 1999 study by the DNR it was determined that
very few fish caught on non-offset circle hooks died.

Physical injury and stress are the two main factors influencing survival of fish that are caught and released. Location of the hook wound is the single most important factor influencing the survival of released fish. In addition, high water temperatures, low salinity and larger fish size has been shown to increase the mortality of released striped bass. Along the Atlantic Coast from Maine to North Carolina, 14.2 million striped bass were caught in 1999 and 90% were released. Assuming an 8% mortality rate, the released striped bass would equal 1.02 million dead fish. Knowing this information, you can appreciate the strong encouragement by the MSSA, DNR and the ASMFC to use circle hooks.

You must change your fishing techniques when using circle hooks. The key is to allow the fish to take in the bait and move off with it. Even if the fish swallows the bait because of the hook being round, it will be pulled up through his stomach without snagging his intestines. However, when the leader is pulled taut and the hook begins to exit the fish, the design will cause the hook to turn at an angle in which it will be hooked into the mouth of the fish. The fish will be hooked 98% of the time in the mouth.

Of course, there are fishermen who will resist anything new or have tried them once and say that they don't work. Fishing with circle hooks is definitely a new style of fishing for most of us. You must allow the fish to take the bait into its mouth and move off with it. If you try to set the hook as you have done in the past, you will jerk the hook out of its mouth. When just starting to use circle hook, you should place your rod in the rod holder. When you see a fish first biting your bait, then is the time to sit on your hands. Don't touch the rod! When the rod is bent and stays bent it is time to grab the rod out of the holder and reel, not jerk, the rod. He is already hooked at this point, so jerking the rod could pull the hook.

After you have caught a few fish by using circle hooks, you can begin to experiment by holding the rod and begin to learn how to raise your rod tip to set the hook. Notice, that I said to raise your rod, not to jerk your rod. I would like to recommend 10/0 or 11/0 circle hooks. Don't buy offset circle hooks because they would defeat your purpose for their use.

I now use circle hooks exclusively. Yes, other captains have out-fished me because they are using conventional hooks and their clients are jerking their rods at every bite. Unfortunately, they are catching a smaller grade of fish by using a smaller hook and smaller bait than I use. Several of those fish are "gut hooked" and will soon become a statistic. Yes, it might swim off when released, but within a few days it will be a floater.

Please allow me to preach to you one more time on the use of circle hooks. Try them! But you must use them exclusively or you must know and must keep track of which rods have circle hooks. Leave them in the rod holders and let them catch the fish for you. Circle hooks are your future. Try not to be hardheaded like I was until a few years ago. After hearing from other fishermen and other charterboat captains on how effective they were in reducing mortality, I forced myself to learn to use them. Now I think these hooks are the greatest things since sliced bread in protecting and preserving our striped bass fishery. If you won't do it for yourself, than do it for your children and grandchildren.

In the box you go!

 # CIRCLE HOOK BAITING MADE EASY

1. Start with a good work area and equipment. This cutting board conveniently fits into any rod holder and the work surface can be adjusted to any angle. I use two knives; one has an offset handle and serrated blade. The second knife is used to puncture a hole for your hook.

2. The serrated blade knife is great for cutting those frozen baits all season without dulling the blade.

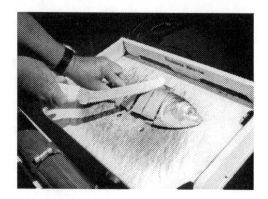

3. Using the serrated blade knife, cut off the head and tail sections and cut your baits approximately 1-1/2 inches wide.

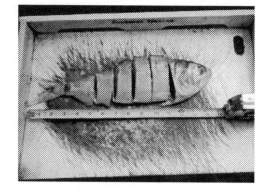

4. Using a sharp pointed knife or an ice pick, puncture your bait in order to make insertion of your circle hook easier.

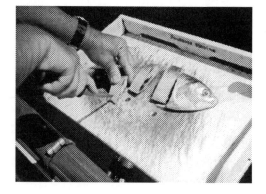

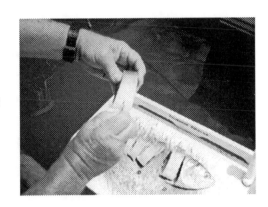

5. Guide the circle hook through the puncture hole and out the other side of the skin.

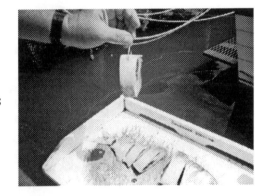

6. Circle hooks should be hooked through both sides of the bait.

Using large pieces of bait will improve the quality of your catch. *"Big Bait - Big Fish"*! Try using no weight on a couple of your lines and as the tide increases, add an ounce or two of weight. Fish your baits well behind your boat at first. But once you have fish in your chum line, you may want to fish a couple of lines directly underneath the boat. You may be pleasantly surprised.

Using gloves will protect your hands from leader line cuts and
minimize slime loss to the fish

 # CAREFUL CATCH

*Credit - Article written by Maryland Department of Natural Resources
and printed by permission.*

Catch & Release

Effective "*catch & release*" is essential to the future of fishing in the
Chesapeake Bay. Whether fishermen choose to release fish or are
required to do so by law, all released fish must be handled carefully to
have a good chance for survival.

Under the right conditions, a good angler can guarantee that more
than 90 percent of the fish released will survive. The fisherman
controls four factors that affect a fish's chance of survival:

- *Exhaustion* - The fight is tough on the fish. It can upset the fish's chemical balance if it lasts too long.

- *Loss of Slime* - Fish are cloaked in a coat of slime which serves the same function as our skin, by sealing out infection. Rough handling can destroy the slime layer, making the fish vulnerable to infection.

- *Time Out of The Water* - As long as it is out of the water, a fish can't breathe or restore its chemical balance after a tough fight.

- *Wounds* - Anglers can do a lot to minimize the damage of hook wounds both before and after the fish is hooked.

<u>Planning Ahead</u>

Use strong enough tackle. Many fishermen like to use light tackle because some consider it to be more sporting, but any fish you plan to release should be brought to the boat quickly to minimize exhaustion.

Use artificial baits whenever possible. Fish tend to swallow natural baits, while they are usually hooked in the lip or mouth with artificial baits. A lip wound is much less severe than a gut wound.

Set the hook quickly when using natural bait so the fish does not have time to swallow.

<u>Ideal Release</u>

Use a de-hooker to remove a hook quickly, keeping the fish in or over the water. There will be little or no slime loss or time out of the water. You can make or buy a de-hooker.

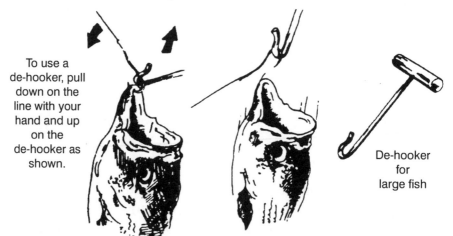

To use a de-hooker, pull down on the line with your hand and up on the de-hooker as shown.

De-hooker for large fish

If you must remove the fish from the water

Remove the fish carefully by supporting its weight in an upright position with your hand and lifting straight up; or

Keep control of the fish so that it cannot flop around the deck and cause further wounds or loss of slime.

Handling and releasing the fish

Handle fish carefully using wet cotton gloves or a wet towel to minimize slime loss. If you must use your hands, be sure to wet them first.

Always avoid touching the gills. This is where the fish takes in oxygen and salts from the water when recovering from the exhaustion of the fight. Gills are very delicate.

Carefully return the fish to the water after removing the hook. Hold it in or close to the water and release it upright and head first.

When the hook is in the gut or gill, cut the line close to the fish's mouth and leave the hook. It may or may not rust out, but trying to remove it may make the wound fatal. Fish will sometimes expel hooks or surround them with tough tissues, minimizing further wounding. Look for new de-hookers designed for handling gut hooked fish.

Jeff chumming off the *"Hill"* in 2000
captured this striper in 39 feet of water

1999 STRIPED BASS CIRCLE HOOK STUDY

Credit - Article written by Maryland DNR Fisheries Biologist Rudy Lukaovic and printed by permission.

Introduction

The popularity of *"catch and release"* fishing for striped bass has increased substantially in recent years. Along the Atlantic Coast from Maine to North Carolina, 14.2 million striped bass were caught in 1999 and 90% were released. An assumed constant 8% mortality rate for released striped bass is incorporated into state and federal management plans to set seasons and limits. Therefore, the mortality of released fish can be a significant component of overall fishing mortality.

Since 1996, the Fisheries Service of the Maryland Department of Natural Resources has been conducting studies that evaluate factors that influence the survival of fish that are caught and released by recreational anglers. Studies have included hickory and American shad, white perch, summer flounder and striped bass.

Physical injury and stress are the two main factors influencing survival of fish that are caught and released. Fish can be physically injured from hook wounds and during handling and release. They can be physiologically stressed by the exertion from the fight.

Numerous studies with a variety of species have shown that the location of the hook wound, is the single most important factor influencing the survival of released fish. If the wound site is a vital organ, mortality is high. The wound site can be affected by hook size or configuration, bait size, the use of natural bait verses artificial lures (natural baits tend to be swallowed more frequently), angler experience or fish behavior.

Stress-related mortality can be affected by variations in the environment. Temperature, salinity and fish size are three important and interactive factors that affect survival of caught and released striped bass. High temperatures, low salinity and larger fish size have been shown to increase, individually or in combination, the mortality of released striped bass.

Methods

The Fisheries Service conducted a study that evaluated the survival of striped bass caught on conventional hooks and circle hooks in different environmental conditions in the Chesapeake Bay. The study was conducted with the cooperation of the Maryland Charter Boat Association, the Maryland Coastal Conservation Association and the Maryland Saltwater Sportfishermen's Association.

- Striped bass were caught by hook and line at Love Point at the mouth of the Chester River and at the Diamonds near the Choptank River.

- They were held in pens off Love Point and at the Cooperative Oxford Laboratory. (See adjacent page for map of the fishing and net pen locations.

- Two 2-day trials were conducted at each location from June through October.

- Conventional bait hooks were used the first day and similar sized, non-offset circle hooks were used the second day.

- Fifty striped bass was the target number for each day. Striped bass were caught by chumming and anglers were instructed to hook, play and land the fish in a normal manner.

- The location of the hook wound was identified when each fish was landed.

- Fisheries Service biologists removed the hook if the fish was shallow hooked, but left the hook in place in deep hooked fish by cutting the line.

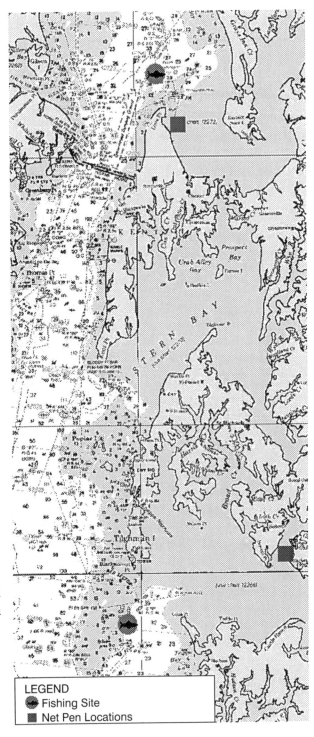

LEGEND
● Fishing Site
■ Net Pen Locations

- Each fish was marked to identify hook location (shallow or deep) by hole punching the tail fin.

- The fish were placed in tanks on board DNR transport vessels.

- Oxygen, temperature and salinity measurements from surface, mid-water and bottom depths were taken at each site several times each day.

- The most optimal conditions for survival (lowest temperature and highest oxygen) found at each site were duplicated in the tank.

- When 25 fish were captured, they were transported to the net-pens.

- The striped bass were held for 72 hours and checked daily for mortality.

- Temperature, dissolved oxygen and salinity were monitored in the pens each day. Dead fish were measured and had hook location recorded.

- All dead fish, marked as deep hooked, were dissected to determine the nature and extent of the internal damage that caused death.

- All surviving fish were measured, had hook location recorded and were released after 72 hours.

Results

- Anglers caught 476 striped bass with conventional bait hooks and 640 with non-offset circle hooks.

- The size of striped bass caught with bait hooks were similar (16.7 in.; 10.5 - 36.6 in.) to those fish caught with non-offset circle hooks (16.4. in; 11.4 - 36.3 in.).

- The deep hooking rate for conventional bait hooks over the course of the entire study was 17.2% and was 3.4% for non-offset circle hooks. This large decrease in deep hooking has been documented in several other Fisheries Service studies (24% for conventional hooks vs. 4% for circle hooks in summer 1996 and 46% vs. 11% in spring 1997).

- The deep hooking mortality rate for striped bass caught with conventional bait hooks in this study was 53.1%. The deep hooking mortality rate with non-offset circle hooks was 23.5%.

Studies done here in Maryland have consistently shown the deep hooking mortality rate of striped bass caught with conventional bait hooks to be about 50% regardless of temperature or salinity (57.7% in 1995; 41.0% in 1996 and 56.3% in 1997).

- Overall, 9.1% of the striped bass caught on conventional hooks died whereas only 0.8% of the fish caught on circle hooks died.

Discussion

Post mortem examinations of deep hooked striped bass caught with conventional bait hooks showed hook points penetrating heart and/or liver in most dead fish, and severe internal hemorrhage in all dead, deep hooked fish, even when major organs had not been penetrated. Post mortem dissections of fish deep hooked with circle hooks showed tears in the esophagus were caused by not the point, but by the outside bend of the hook. Non-offset circle hooks orient the point away from the direction of travel when the line is pulled tight. The point does not penetrate organs as a conventional bait hook with its point facing the direction of travel. Long term survival of deep hooked fish is not well documented.

Shallow hooking is defined as those fish hooked in the mouth. A profound effect on shallow hooking mortality was documented in relation to air temperature. When air temperatures were below 95 degrees F, the mortality of shallow hooked striped bass, those fish only stressed by physical exertion not by lethal hook wounds, was 0.8%. When air temperatures ranged from 95 to 105 degrees F in July, mortality rose to 17.2%. The mortality rate of all shallow hooked fish combined was 3.5% for the entire study period.

Death in these studies is rapid. More than 75% of the fish that die, die in less than 6 hours and 95% die in less than 24 hours. Other catch-and-release studies with striped bass, shad and white perch show the same mortality pattern. This strongly suggests that mortality of these fish reflects hooking injury or angling stress, not confinement because mortality is rapid and usually associated with severe internal damage from hook damage. Mortality from caging stress would be expressed over time as fish languished in confinement. All fish that survive in the net pens are extremely vigorous at release.

Catch and release mortality studies in Maryland have shown that under most circumstances catch and release fishing is a relatively conservative practice. However there are circumstances under which release mortality can be high.

In the 1999 study, we determined that 9.1% of the fish caught on conventional hooks died, but only 0.8% of the fish caught on circles hooks died. This dramatic difference in mortality should encourage anglers and fishery resource managers to strive to reduce deep hooking rates. Non-offset circle hooks not only reduce frequency of deep hooking, but deep hooking mortality is lower with non-offset circle hooks than conventional bait hooks.

When environmental conditions are stressful for released fish (high temperature, both air and water, and low salinity) anglers should minimize catch-and-release fishing. When angling during periods of extreme air temperatures (>95 degrees F) keep the fish in the water when releasing. In 1999 we had also intended to evaluate release mortality at two significantly different salinity levels. Drought conditions this summer prevented mortality trials from being conducted at low salinity sites. An identical study will be done in the summer of 2000 to evaluate striped bass catch and release mortality under a low salinity environment.

 # WHAT HAPPENS TO THE HOOKS?

*Credit - Article written by John Foster of the Maryland DNR
and printed per permission.*

<u>True or False</u>

*When a fish takes a hook deep, just cut the leader and the hook will
rust or fall out in a couple of days and it doesn't hurt the fish.*

This myth is still believed by many anglers and writers but recent
studies tell a different story, that:

(1) hooks do not rust or fall out, and

(2) hooks left in the throat of fish will eventually kill them.

Scientists are now saying to remove deep hooks whenever possible.

Several years ago biologists began questioning the traditional thinking that hooks rust out quickly and that hooks left in the throat or gut do not harm the fish. If this were so, why do human doctors treat internal throat and esophagus injuries with hospitalization? Why shouldn't a similar injury to a fish be as life threatening?

Recent studies by the Maryland Fisheries Division at the Oxford Cooperative Laboratory addressed the question of what happens to hooks left in fish. Striped bass of various sizes were hooked deep in their throat or esophagus with stainless, tin plated, nickel plated or "bronzed" hooks. Four months later 78% of the hooks were still in the fish with no difference between material type. The hooks that rusted off, did so at the area on the shank where the hook entered the throat tissue and left a "nubbin" protruding into the throat.

The immediate survival of hooked fish is determined primarily by hooking location. The area around the throat contains the heart, liver and head kidney. If a hook point becomes lodged or significantly damages one of these organs, the fish will probably die shortly.

Normally the hook becomes embedded in the thick, muscular throat tissues where the fibroma or scar tissue forms around it. This is a normal healing response for fish which may receive similar injuries from the spines or bones of things they eat. When this scar tissue forms around the barb, the hook is essentially locked in place in a walled off pocket.

But does the hook harm the fish? Yes and no. The striped bass in the Maryland studies were feeding 24 hours after being hooked and behave normally throughout the study and as long as they were in ideal conditions. When the fish runs into stressful conditions, the health of the fish may be effected. Subsequent observations found latent mortality caused by extensive bacterial infections around the walled off hook. The Maryland fish started to die from bacterial infections around the hook in the spring following the study. Apparently a major stress on the fish such as spawning or abnormally high water temperatures will permit a break down of internal defenses and allow the infection to overtake the fish. These abscesses will probably form around hooks left deep in any fish at sometime when suitable environmental and stress conditions coincide.

A recent study in Holland with deep hooked pike found a 86% survival rate after 110 months when hooks were cut off and left in the throat. This compared to 98% survival of pike with hooks removed. Similarly, the Maryland work had 91-98% survival of their deep hooked striped bass.

Mortality rates for deeply hooked fish are significant. The overall effect on the species stock varies with the portion of fish caught which break off or are released with hooks in their throats. A Georgia study of hook caught red drum found that 10% of the fish were hooked in the esophagus with a survival rate of 50% with hook left in place. This compared to an 89% survival for drum hooked in the gills and jaw. A Texas study on red drum and spotted seatrout with all hooks removed found 96% and 93% respective survival.

Many fisheries biologists are now recommending removal of all hooks from fish before releasing. Various de-hooking tools are available ranging from the simple to the complex. The most effective and simplest de-hooker I have found for removing single hooks is one made by two former commercial hook and line fishermen whose conscience got to them. Their "Deep Throat De-Hookers" allow quick and easy removal of hooks, especially deep hooks previously cut off. Most important, it allows the hooks to be removed while the fish is still in the water. By not taking the fish out of the water, especially in warm weather, handling is reduced, stress is minimized, and the fisherman is fishing again sooner.

The "Deep Throat De-Hooker" is produced in several sizes to match hook sizes for everything from pan fish (#4 hook) to sharks, tuna and marlin (12/0 +). It is an essential item when chumming and releasing stripers, bluefish and tuna. The "Deep Throat De-Hooker" is available from many tackle shops, and the Chesapeake Bay Foundation (1-800-728-5229). Like most tools, practice using it at home before trying it on fish.

A good de-hooker not only increases the survival rate of your released fish, but by unhooking fish faster, you spend more time fishing. Isn't that why we go?

On the following page, please note the release survival rates of several fish.

Release Survival Rates of Several Fish

Type: ....Striped Bass
From: ....Massachusetts
Length: ....11 to 22 inches
Hook Location: .... Out
Survival %: 98
Time: ....2 Months

Type: ....Striped Bass
From: ....Maryland
Length: ....18 to 28 inches
Hook Location: ....In Deep
Survival %: ....91 to 98
Time: ....4 Months

Type: ....Pike
From: ....Holland
Length: ....22 to 32 inches
Hook Location: ....Out Deep ....In Deep
Survival %: ....98..............................86
Time: ....10 Months

Type: ....Red Drum
From: ....Georgia
Length: ....less than 14 inches
Hook Location: ....Out Jaw, Gill ....In Deep
Survival %: ....89..............................50
Time: ....14 Days

Type: ....Red Drum
From: ....Texas
Length: ....16 to 33 inches
Hook Location: ....Out
Survival %: 96
Time: ....3 Days

Type: ....Spotted Seatrout
From: ....Texas
Length: ....9 to 19 inches
Hook Location: ....Out
Survival %: 93
Time: ....3 Days

 # DO YOUR RELEASED FISH LIVE?

Credit - Article written by John Foster of the Maryland DNR
and printed per permission.

It's a warm afternoon with a light breeze and you have been casting a bucktail along the shore. Fishing has been good, the fish have been running 3 to 8 pounds, really burning the drag on that new light tackle outfit, you have gotten some good photos showing off your catches, and you feel good having released all your fish.

But, do your releases live?

Catch and release fishing is becoming more common as more anglers seek fishing as a sport or recreational activity and legal restrictions limit the size and number of fish kept. Anglers need to learn more about how to successfully release their catch. To assist in this effort, many states have conducted studies aimed to improve our understanding of why fish die following release, and to determine ways to reduce mortality that can be taught to anglers. It is felt that education rather than regulations is the key to successful catch and release programs.

What is it that kills fish that have been released?

Usually it is a combination of factors that include exhaustion, lack of oxygen, time out of water, handling and sometimes injury. When a fish is brought to the side of the boat and slowly rolls on its side, it is exhausted. The fish is picked up, measured, the hook is removed and pictures of the angler and fish are taken. The fish is returned to its world, the angler *"pumps"* water through the gills and the fish slowly swims off.

But does it survive?

From the moment the fish was hooked to when it reached the boat, the fish has been expending tremendous amounts of energy to escape. Its energy reserves are low and like a runner, muscles may begin to cramp and the oxygen levels are becoming dangerously low. Every second out of the water, its condition is getting worse. Without water flowing over the gills, most fish cannot breathe. The by-products of extreme exercise, lactic acid and carbon dioxide and low oxygen quickly begin to damage tissues and *"shock"* can soon set it. Though the fish was seen swimming off, internal damages may be too great for the fish to overcome and death may come several days later.

How Long Out of The Water?

Time out of the water varies with temperature and stress on the fish. A guide is available from a Canadian study using rainbow trout. The fish were exercised to exhaustion at a moderate temperature for trout. One group was left in the water, a second group was exposed to air for 30 seconds and the third group was in air for 60 seconds. All the fish were alive and swimming when returned to the water. After three days, 12% of those left in the water died, while 38% in the 30 second group and 72% for those out of water for 60 seconds. While this study was not in the *"real world"*, its results indicate the importance of returning fish to the water quickly.

Why might this be happening?

The fish need a continual supply of oxygenated water flowing through its gills to remove the high carbon dioxide in the blood and replace it with oxygen. When the fish is removed from the water, the oxygen is shut off and the CO_2 and lactic acid build up rapidly to levels that may damage the gills and other tissues such as the brain.

Importance of Environmental Conditions

The primary environmental factor affecting survival of released fish is water temperature, according to work done at Maryland DNR's Cooperative Oxford Laboratory. Several studies were done to find the effects of water temperature and salinity on the survival of angled striped bass. When the water temperature was above 70 degrees F. mortality associated with hooking stress increased significantly. Salinity may have an effect on stress, but is overridden by temperature.

The size of the fish caught at warmer temperatures is also important to survival. Because the ratio of surface area to overall volume decreases with the increasing size of a fish, it is harder for large fish to get rid of excess by-products of exercise or gain sufficient oxygen. This means that when a large fish is played hard, it may be affected more by by-product build-up from exercise than smaller fish. In striped bass, fish over about 25 inches may be more prone to such problems than smaller ones.

The combination of temperature and size as shown in Figure 1 indicates the effect of temperature and size on survival of "angled" striped bass in lab conditions. While the mortality rates of smaller fish (<18 inches) at all temperatures is within the ASMFC 8% by-catch estimate, the mortality of larger fish (>22 inches) in warm water (>70 degrees) is 16 to 22%. The mortality rates seen in the real world will vary due to different environmental conditions and stresses on fish.

Figure 1 - Percent Mortality of Laboratory "Angled" Striped Bass at Different Temperatures

	Smalls <18 inches	Larges >22 inches
Cool water, < 70 degrees F	4 - 6%	0.5 - 2%
Warm water, > 70 degrees F	2 - 4%	16 - 22%

When To Be More Careful

In the Chesapeake Bay, the average surface water temperature moves above 70 degrees in mid-June and normally stays in the upper 70's until September. Bays like the Chesapeake usually have uniform temperature from top to bottom in summer. In coastal areas, though water temperatures in shallows get warm, there usually are cooler waters in deeper channels for fish to take refuge.

The Angler Can Make A Difference

While environmental conditions can have an effect on survival, it is the angler's handling that has the greatest effect on survival of released fish. By practicing a few simple catch and release principles, fishermen can still enjoy the catch and be assured their release will survive to be enjoyed by another fisherman.

1. Be prepared, have all equipment ready: de-hooker, camera, etc.
2. Use heavy enough tackle to get fish in quickly.
3. Keep fish in the water.
4. If necessary, no more than 15 seconds out of the water.
5. Be more careful, when water is warm.

 # DEEP THROAT DE-HOOKER

While fishing during the June striped bass fishery, I had the opportunity to use a new device for dislodging hooks out of deep hooked rockfish. The device that I am referring to is called the *Deep Throat De-Hooker.*

I was given this tool by Mr. John Foster, a biologist for the Department of Natural Resources. John asked me to give this new device a try during the spring fishery. Due to the minimum size limit of 18 inches during the May trophy season I elected not to chum fearing the mortality rate would be too high. I did, however, chum for stripers during the June fishery since the minimum size was lowered to 18 inches. After using the *Deep Throat De-Hooker* on my first chumming trip, I was "*hooked*". The *Deep Throat De-Hooker* allowed me to remove a deep hooked hook out of a fish without removing it from the water, thus causing little harm to the fish.

In a recent article written by Mr. John Foster of the DNR, he stated that survival rate dramatically increases when hooks are removed from a fish. In several recent studies, the "*Old Wives' Tale*" that a hook left in a fish will rust or corrode out in a few days has been proven false. Studies indicate hooks do not rust or fall out and hooks left in the throat of fish eventually kill them. Scientist are now advising to remove deep hooks whenever possible.

I was really impressed with how effective this device was in removing hooks that were swallowed or lodged deep in the rockfish throat. It allows you to leave the fish in the water while removing the hook. This means that you don't have to handle the fish, therefore you won't be removing its protective slime or mucus that protects the fish from disease.

The *Deep Throat De-Hooker* is very easy to use. Slide the tool down your line to the lodged hook, with a push of the tool into the fish mouth while holding the leader line, the hook is automatically dislodged. It's that simple!

I'm sure that many of you will be eeling or chumming during the season. I highly recommend that you purchase the *Deep Throat De-Hooker* if you are planning to fish using either of these two methods. Not only does this tool easily remove a hook that is embedded deep in the fish's throat or gullet, but will increase the survival of the fish you release.

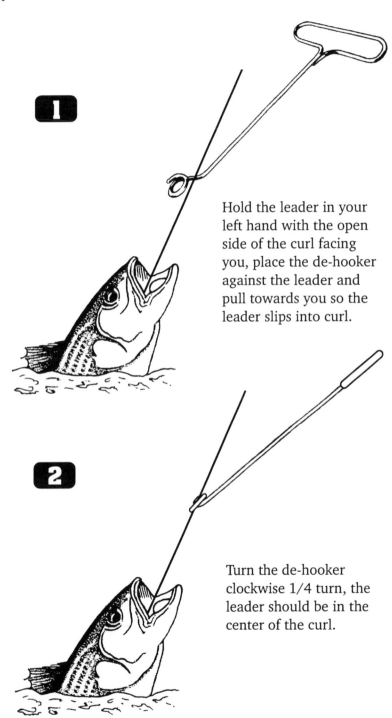

1

Hold the leader in your left hand with the open side of the curl facing you, place the de-hooker against the leader and pull towards you so the leader slips into curl.

2

Turn the de-hooker clockwise 1/4 turn, the leader should be in the center of the curl.

HOW TO USE A DE-HOOKER

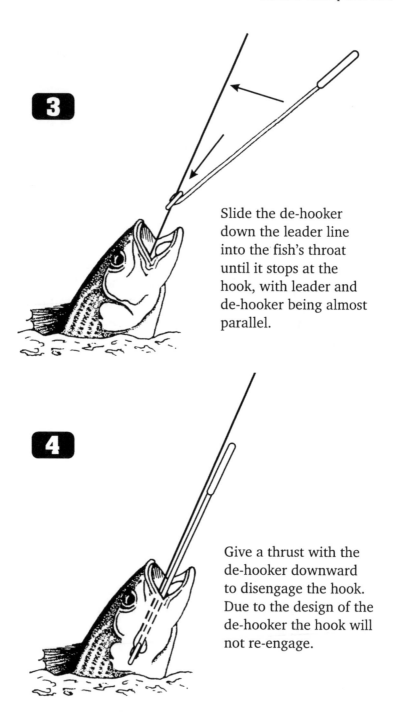

3 Slide the de-hooker down the leader line into the fish's throat until it stops at the hook, with leader and de-hooker being almost parallel.

4 Give a thrust with the de-hooker downward to disengage the hook. Due to the design of the de-hooker the hook will not re-engage.

HOW TO USE A DE-HOOKER

 **HOOK OUT**

Regardless of your method of fishing, a hook is part of your lure. As we all know, accidents do happen. If a barbed hook is involved it can be painful, dangerous and will most certainly cause the end of a nice day of fishing.

The following is a certified method of removing a hook from human flesh. It can be done with on-board material or you can buy an inexpensive kit. Either way, it is a procedure we should all be familiar with. It's best to be prepared and hope you never have to use it.

Stay safe, stay healthy and stay fishing.

This is the same method recognized and taught by fishing clinics and emergency rooms around the country as being the best and least painful way of removing a barbed fishhook in almost all cases.

You have a number of choices. First if the lure is still attached to the fish (or anything else for that matter), clip the line to free the lure. Sometimes you can continue to push the hook all the way through the wound and out again. This action is somewhat painful but it is sometimes doable.

Another method, favored by many anglers, looks as if it shouldn't work, but it does. You need to have some confidence in this method or you may not do very well. Try practicing this on a piece of raw meat until you understand what you are doing. After you get the idea, it all makes sense.

REMOVING A HOOK

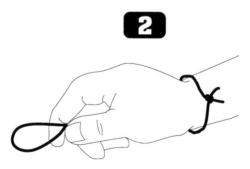

Take a two foot length of at least 25-pound test line and tie the ends together so that you have a loop. If you do not have 25 lb. test line, then double a few strands of 10 lb. or 12 lb. test line.

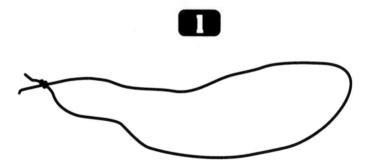

Loop the line over your wrist and form a small loop between your thumb and forefinger.

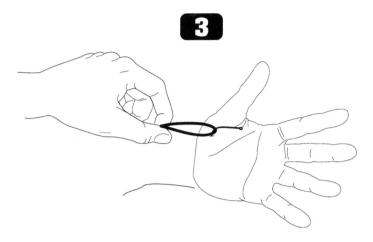

Take this small loop and put it around the hook in the center of the hook's bend.

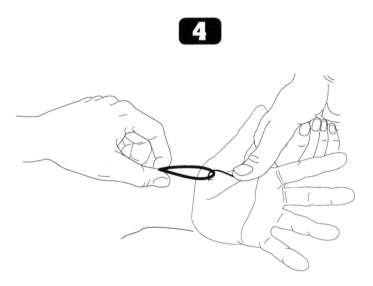

With your other thumb press down on the eye of the hook. This action should open the wound enough for you to gently back the barb out of your flesh. Getting the barb clear of the flesh is very important. If you do not get the barb clear, you should not continue with this procedure.

Finally, pull on the small loop with a sharp jerk. The hook should come free with relatively little pain.

This striper fell to Ray Mosca's umbrella rig in the fall of 2003 off Love Point

TRADITIONAL FALL TROLLING FOR ROCKFISH IN THE UPPER BAY

One of the traditional methods used to fish for striped bass is trolling. Trolling for rockfish in the fall has been a proven technique since the turn of the century. Trolling enables you to cover more fishing area in the shortest amount of time. It enables you to find fish either feeding on the bottom or while they are suspended in the water column.

Beginning in September the Bay's water will begin to cool. This cooling effect of the water will begin to trigger the mechanism in rockfish that makes them school and feed aggressively in order to build up their *"fat"* that will be necessary to survive the winter. By mid-October through December, they have schooled and are actively

feeding throughout the Bay. The
exciting part about trolling for
rockfish in the fall is that you are
holding your rod, if bottom
bouncing, when the fish hits your
line. Believe me, sometimes it feels
like the fish is going to jerk the rod right
out of your hand because of hitting the line
so aggressively.

While fall trolling, using a much larger size lure than the traditional size pays off.

You will be allowed to possess two
rockfish per day during the season. The
minimum size limit will still be 18 inches.

Traditionally, 1/0 to 3/0 bucktails were used
to target rockfish in the fall in the Upper Bay. The
reason that these small bucktails were used was
because the size limit at that time was only 12 inches. Now with a
larger minimum size limit of 18 inches, I would recommend that you
use a larger size lure. Usually I stopped eel fishing in mid-October and
I started trolling through the end of the season. My most productive
lures trolling were bucktails, parachutes, sassy shads and Crippled
Alewives. One thing that I did during this season was to use a much
larger size lure than the traditional sizes that I mentioned earlier. I was
using 5/0 to 7/0 bucktails and 9/0 Crippled Alewives. Every fish I
caught was larger than the 18 inch minimum size limit. In fact, I never
caught a fish smaller than 20 inches. Although several other boats
fishing in the same area were catching and releasing smaller undersize fish, I didn't because I was using larger size artificial lures. On
several occasions I used a 6 inch sassy shad that was very
productive. Since the use of plastics has evolved in the last
decade, dressing your bucktail with a sassy shad or twister
tail - is the way to go. These plastic
twister tails are so much easier to use
and discard at the end of the day than
the traditional pork rind. If you have
ever forgotten to take off the pork
rind at the end of the day - you will
know what I'm talking about.

Now that I have suggested what lures to use, let's talk about equipment. I prefer a 20 or 30 lb. class rod, 6 to 6-1/2 feet, medium to medium heavy action. My choice or reels are Penn 309s or 330 GTIs filled with 30 lb. test of Monel wire (single strand) or the new synthetic lines such as spider wire, gorilla or power pro spectra line. I use a 40 to 50 lb. test monofilament leader line of 18 feet in overall length.

Rigging your line is the next important thing that I would like to address. Always use a shock leader between your wire line, off your reel and your snap swivel. I like to use a 60 lb. test monofilament line for this shock leader. I then place a three-way swivel onto my snap swivel. On one of the two remaining circles, I tie a 30 inch drop line of 25 lb. test for my sinker. I generally like to place a snap swivel at the end, so that I am able to change to a different weight depending on the tide, current and depth of water throughout the day, without cutting my line. On the third circle of my three-way swivel, I tie on a 18 foot 50 pound test monofilament line for my leader. Then tie the lure directly onto the line.

A good depth finder is essential. You must have the ability to read underwater structures. This could be an artificial fishing reef, a sunken boat or a sharp drop-off, where the rockfish is waiting for small baitfish and tidbits that are being washed down these shoals because of the tide and current. It is very important to have a moving tide, either ebb or flood. As long as you have a tide you should be able to catch fish. On occasion I have seen rockfish feed so aggressively, that I was able to catch them all day long, regardless of what the tide was doing.

I never start to fish unless I see the fish on my depth finder. I may ride around for an hour or more before I locate the fish. Once they are located, I mark the spot with a marker or punch the location into my GPS.

Boat speed is very important in fishing for rockfish. The slower the better, is the way to go. You want just enough horsepower to move the boat forward while you are bouncing your bait across the bottom. If you cannot go this slow, try fishing against the tide to slow your boat down or pull a five-gallon bucket behind your boat, to help you slow down.

The following illustration depicts my trolling rig, better known as a *"bottom bouncing"* trolling rig. It is very important that you are able to feel the bottom with your weight at all times. You want to be able to lift your weight slightly off the bottom by moving your rod and then ease your weight back again. Leave only enough line out to keep your weight in contact with the bottom. The fish are on the bottom feeding.

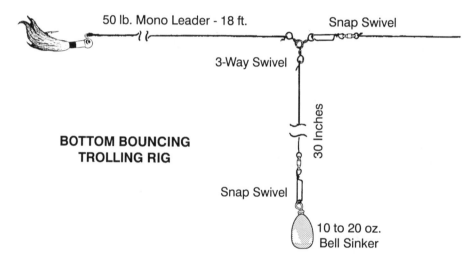

Another popular trolling rig is the double rig. Attach a three-way swivel to your running line off of your reel. Next attach a 30 inch, 25 lb. test drop sinker line on one of your three-way circles. Be sure to place a snap swivel on the tag end to make changing weights easier. On the last ring tie on a 12 foot monofilament leader line of 40 to 50 lb. test and then tie that tag end to another three-way swivel. Measure off 3 feet of 40 lb. test and tie it on one of the remaining circles. Next tie on a six foot piece of 40 lb. test mono on the final ring. Now you can tie on your two lures and you have just doubled your chances to catch that rockfish.

Finally, I would like to address the proper handling of rockfish that you catch. Try to handle them as little as possible. Use a de-hooker

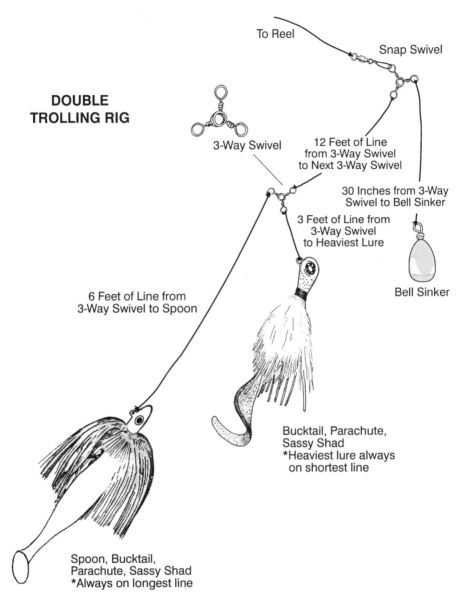

DOUBLE TROLLING RIG

To Reel

Snap Swivel

3-Way Swivel

12 Feet of Line
from 3-Way Swivel
to Next 3-Way Swivel

30 Inches from 3-Way
Swivel to Bell Sinker

3 Feet of Line from
3-Way Swivel
to Heaviest Lure

Bell Sinker

6 Feet of Line from
3-Way Swivel to Spoon

Bucktail, Parachute,
Sassy Shad
*Heaviest lure always
on shortest line

Spoon, Bucktail,
Parachute, Sassy Shad
*Always on longest line

whenever possible, if you are not going to keep the fish. Usually the fish are lip-hooked during trolling. If you do not use a de-hooker, grab the fish by the lower jaw and apply pressure, just as in bass fishing. This will calm the fish enough to remove the hook. Try not place your hands on their body. This will remove the protective film or slime that they use to combat disease. Always use a wet towel or wet your hands when handling fish to be released.

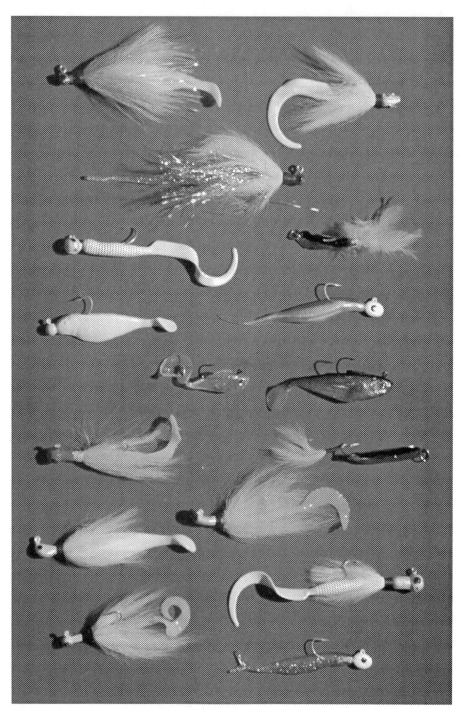

Bottom Bouncing Baits

A fall rockfish caught off of the *"Triple Buoys"* outside the Chester River

 **BOTTOM BOUNCING TIP**

One form of trolling for rockfish is called bottom bouncing. This method is where you allow your weight to bounce off the bottom as you troll your lures behind. You must hold your rod since you will be constantly reeling in or letting out line as you maintain contact with an irregular bottom with your sinker.

Generally, when you are bottom bouncing you are using several size of weights. Bell sinkers are the most commonly used style. Depending on the number of rods being trolled, depth and speed will determine the size of your sinker. Most anglers use 10, 12, 16 or 20 ounce sinkers and occasionally 24 and 28 ounce sinkers, as well. After these sinkers have been used only once, it is extremely difficult to see the imprinted weight size of the sinker. When used again, it's very hard to tell a 10 from a 12 ounce or a 16 ounce from a 20 ounce.

A simple remedy is to mark the different size by using a color code system. This can be easily done by getting several pieces of colored wire (24 to 18 gauge). Telephone wire works great since it already has several different color wires inside one cable. Usually they are red, yellow, black and green in color. Cut off a piece of wire approximately an inch to and inch and a half in length. Next, twist the red wire around the terminal end of your sinker on all of your 10 ounce weights. Now, twist the yellow wire on all of your 12 ounce weights, green wire on all of your 16 ounce weights, and black wire on all of your 20 ounce weights. For my 24 and 28 ounce sinkers, I revert back to red and yellow wires since you can easily tell a 10 ounce weight from a 24 ounce weight. Now you can grab the exact size weight you desire. An easy way to remember this is to think of a traffic signal - red, yellow and green.

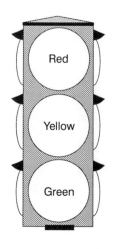

Red
Yellow
Green
Black
An easy way to remember this is to think of a traffic signal

COLOR CODE YOUR WEIGHTS

Twist red wire around terminal end of all your 10 ounce weights

Twist yellow wire around terminal end of all your 12 ounce weights

Twist green wire around terminal end of all your 16 ounce weights

Twist black wire around terminal end of all your 20 ounce weights

 # STRIPED BASS
LENGTH-WEIGHT CHART

Length	Age	Maximum Lbs.	Average Lbs.	Minimum Lbs.
12	1	1.00	1.00	1.00
13	1	2.00	1.50	1.00
14	2	2.50	2.25	2.00
15	2	3.00	2.50	2.00
16	2	3.50	3.00	2.50
17	3	4.00	3.50	2.75
18	3	4.50	4.00	3.00
19	3	5.00	4.25	3.50

Length	Age	Maximum Lbs.	Average Lbs.	Minimum Lbs.
20	3	5.50	4.75	4.00
21	4	6.00	5.00	4.25
22	4	6.75	5.75	4.75
23	4	7.50	6.25	5.00
24	5	8.25	7.00	6.00
25	5	8.80	7.80	6.30
26	6	10.00	8.50	7.00
27	6	11.00	9.80	8.00
28	6	12.00	10.30	8.75
29	7	12.90	11.00	9.70
30	7	14.00	12.25	10.30
31	8	15.00	13.00	11.00
32	8	16.70	14.50	12.00
33	9	17.80	15.80	13.00
34	9	19.00	16.50	14.00
35	10	20.50	18.00	15.50
36	10	22.00	19.50	16.80
37	11	23.50	20.70	17.50
38	12	25.50	22.00	19.00
39	12	27.20	24.50	20.70
40	13	29.50	26.00	22.00
41	13	31.00	27.30	23.00
42	14	33.50	29.70	25.00
43	14	36.30	32.00	27.00
44	15	39.00	34.00	29.50
45	15	41.00	36.00	30.50
46	16	44.00	38.70	32.50
47	16	47.50	42.00	35.00
48	17	51.00	44.00	37.00
49	17	54.00	47.00	39.00

FALL/WINTER TROLLING IN THE MID-CHESAPEAKE BAY

In November and the first part of December, we have a golden opportunity to capture a trophy rockfish. These rockfish are part of the migratory stock that takes up residence along the East Coast. During their fall migration after leaving New England, they travel south to their winter quarters off of North Carolina. During this migration, many stripers visit the Chesapeake Bay to forage for food.

Now is the time to switch over to those rods, reels and lures that you used in the spring fishery for rockfish. I move my boat down from Middle River to the Rod & Reel Dock in Chesapeake Beach to take advantage of capturing a trophy striper. These trophy bass travel as far north as the Bay Bridges; however, you have more of an advantage to capture one of these beasts if you fish below Chesapeake Beach.

Once again, this is straight away or blind trolling. Set up your lines as trolling during the spring fishery. However, I would suggest adding additional weight to get your lures a little deeper in the water column. You don't need to bottom bounce during this fishery. Large bucktails, parachutes, spoons and umbrella rigs that you used in the spring fishery are the correct choices. Quite often these fish will follow the main shipping channel up the Bay.

Watch for the birds working over these large schools of breaking fish. In fact, look closely at the birds, usually sea gulls, working over the school. This may sound weird, but you can tell the size of fish by the size of the birds working over them. I very seldom stop if I see small birds like terns or juvenile seagulls. However, if I see large seagulls, called gannets, you can count on large stripers under them. These gannets follow these stripers down the coast and into the Bay.

Another sure sign that you are capturing the coastal migratory stock is that they will have sea lice attached to their bodies and gills. These sea lice are found mainly in the ocean because of the higher salinity. Although these parasites are usually not deadly to the fish, they do become a nuisance. Sea lice are tolerated by the fish, but they can be detrimental by  weakening their immune systems and can cause infections from bacteria and viruses. Quite often you can capture rockfish on the muddy bottoms as they try to remove these lice from their bodies.

Frequently, you will be able to fish on very mild days in November and December. The idea is to pick your days. Watch the weather forecast and tell your fishing partners to be ready on a day or two's notice. You won't regret leaving your boat in the water or having it ready to go on your trailer. Just dress for the weather. Remember you can always take clothes off once it warms up.

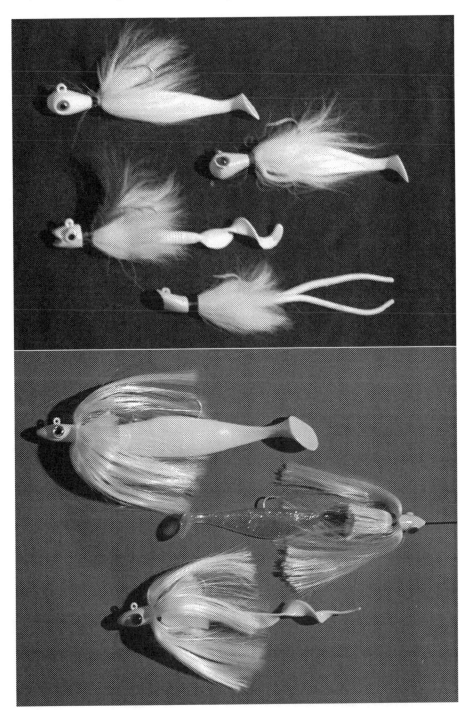

Fall/Winter Trolling Lures - Bucktails & Parachutes

Kevin Geiger with a 48 inch beast caught on an 11/0 Crippled Alewive

 # WHERE ARE ALL OF THE LARGER STRIPED BASS?

Credit - Article written by Maryland Department of Natural Resources and printed by permission

Tagging data has indicated that striped bass incrementally migrate from the Chesapeake Bay to the coastal migrant stock with each passing year. Take a good, close look at the chart. This chart shows you how many striped bass remain in the Chesapeake year round as they age. By age 6 (approximately 24 inches) less than 10% of males and females remain in the bay year round. Where are they? Out on the coast with the migrant stock. The take home message to anglers is that the number of larger fish available to be caught is proportionately much smaller because of this pattern of migration. There are larger fish out there, but there are not nearly as many as there are of the younger fish. We are in somewhat uncharted waters, as we are experiencing the longest sustained level of good production since records were first kept in 1954. It could be that competition for food and space has even further accelerated the migration of these fish to the coastal stock. We continue to tag thousands of striped bass annually with pink streamer tags. The data you return to us helps us better understand the dynamics of striped bass biology and life history. Please report your captured, tagged fish. Fisheries science is a never-ending process of learning, and you can play a major role in that process.

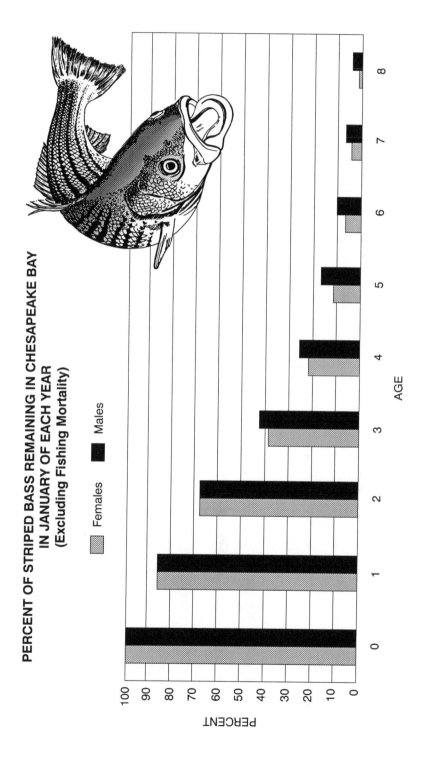

PERCENT OF STRIPED BASS REMAINING IN CHESAPEAKE BAY
IN JANUARY OF EACH YEAR
(Excluding Fishing Mortality)

 # WORKING THE BIRDS

Some of the best fun and excitement you will ever have fishing is working over breaking fish. This phenomenon happens during the summer months, but is more prominent in the fall.

This is a case of predator fish feeding on bait-fish as they schooling. Bait-fish become so disoriented that they will begin to swim to the surface to get away from predators. Unfortunately, for the alewives, rockfish and bluefish will follow them and begin to attach at will at the school. You can actually see the rock and blues tearing through that big ball of baitfish.

A sure telltale sign is working birds over the breaking fish. You should always be on the lookout for birds diving over breaking fish.

Better yet, is to actually see white water from underneath the birds caused by breaking fish. Believe it or not, you can tell with some accountability the size of the rockfish or bluefish by the size of the birds working over them. If you see small white seagulls (terns) working an area, it's usually a sign that they are working over a small grade of rockfish or bluefish. However, if you see large seagulls, gannets or pelicans working over a school of breaking fish, you better stop. Rest assured that a much larger grade of predator fish is working under these birds.

It's best to approach these birds slowly and up-tide whenever possible. If there is a large area that the birds are working, shut down your engine and drift. Killing your engine will allow you to drift with the school and not spook the fish due to engine noise. If the school is sporadic, try to circle the school rather than running directly into the school. This will allow you to keep the fish active and remain near the surface of the water.

Many different lures can be used to cast to these fish. Bucktails, Atom Poppers, Rattletraps, shad bodies rigged on jig heads, Bass Assassins, Storm Lures, silversides, spoons and many others can be used. Cast your lure toward the breaking fish and retrieve it either slowly or fast to see that method works best. You may also want to allow the lure to sink a little further in the water column before retrieving it. This will allow the lure to travel down to larger fish that are lying in wait of cut-up or severed alewives by smaller more aggressive fish near the surface.

Lures to use for breaking fish

Blaine Kurrle holding a trophy rock caught onboard the *"Oh Thank Heaven"*

 # POPULAR FISHING LOCATIONS

Listed below are popular fishing areas. These way-points may not be 100% accurate, but they should be fairly close.

Location	Longitude	Latitude	Map
Abbey Point	N39° 19.93'	W76° 12.57'	Map 1
Worton Point	N39° 19.44'	W76° 11.55'	Map 1
Handys Bar	N39° 17.18'	W76° 13.01'	Map 1
Pooles Island	N39° 16.09'	W76° 15.71'	Map 1
Pooles Island Light	N39° 15.82'	W76° 16.92'	
Shallow Shoal	N39° 16.42'	W76° 14.61'	Map 1

Location	Longitude	Latitude	Map
Miller Island	N39° 15.15'	W76° 19.67'	Map 1
Tolchester	N39° 12.86'	W76° 14.90'	Map 1
Sparty's Lump	N39° 12.67'	W76° 19.17'	Map 1
Hodge's Bar	N39° 11.24'	W76° 16.41'	Map 1
Man of War Shoal	N39° 11.18'	W76° 21.98'	Map 1
Craig Hill Light	N39° 11.16'	W76° 23.93'	Map 1
7 Foot Knoll	N39° 09.30'	W76° 24.50'	Map 1
9 Foot Knoll	N39° 08.75'	W76° 21.87'	Map 2
6 Foot Knoll	N39° 08.62'	W76° 21.89'	Map 2
Swan Point	N39° 07.86'	W76° 19.14'	Map 2
Belvedere Shoal	N39° 06.00'	W76° 22.01'	Map 2
Snake Reef	N39° 06.61'	W76° 25.50'	Map 2
Baltimore Light	N39° 03.50'	W76° 23.90'	Map 2
Love Point	N39° 03.47'	W76° 19.42'	Map 2
L P Buoy	N39° 02.37'	W76° 21.43'	
Podickery Point	N39° 02.10'	W76° 24.01'	Map 2
Sandy Point Light	N39° 01.01'	W76° 23.12'	Map 3
Dumping Grounds	N39° 00.33'	W76° 20.91'	
Winter Hole	N39° 00.14'	W76° 21.65'	
Hackett's Bar	N38° 58.18'	W76° 25.09'	Map 3
Matapeake	N38° 57.64'	W76° 21.89'	Map 3
Brickhouse Bar	N38° 55.46'	W76° 22.02'	
Kentmoor Marina	N38° 54.92'	W76° 22.29'	Map 3
Thomas Point Light	N38° 54.01'	W76° 25.83'	Map 3
Gum Thickets	N38° 52.52'	W76° 23.22'	Map 3
Green Flasher	N38° 51.87'	W76° 27.02'	Map 3
Bloody Point Light	N38° 50.24'	W76° 23.95'	Map 3
Franklin Manor	N38° 49.24'	W76° 30.84'	
The Hill	N38° 46.85'	W° 23.82'	Map 3

Location	Longitude	Latitude	Map
Buoy #83	N38° 45.09'	W76° 26.85'	Map 3
Chesapeake Beach Reef	N38° 42.60'	W76° 29.51'	
Chesapeake Beach	N38° 41.58'	W76° 31.40'	Map 4
Airplane Wreck	N38° 39.60'	W76° 16.01'	Map 4
Sharp Island Light	N38° 39.51'	W76° 22.62'	Map 4
Stone Rock	N38° 39.50'	W76° 23.01'	
C&R Buoy	N38° 38.51'	W76° 25.22'	
Clay Bank	N38° 38.00'	W76° 24.02'	
The Diamonds	N38° 37.03'	W76° 20.21'	
Breezy Point	N38° 36.94'	W76° 30.70'	Map 4
Buoy #80	N38° 36.55'	W76° 24.72'	
Clancy's	N38° 34.67'	W76° 29.41'	Map 4
Buoy #78	N38° 33.30'	W76° 25.69'	
Parker Creek	N38° 32.27'	W76° 29.00'	
Summer Gooses	N38° 31.61'	W76° 23.02'	Map 4
C P Buoy	N38° 28.20'	W76° 22.59'	
Gas Docks	N38° 25.39'	W76° 18.72'	
Cove Point	N38° 23.47'	W76° 22.70'	
Chinese Mud	N38° 19.54'	W76° 22.64'	Map 5
Cedar Point	N38° 18.79'	W76° 22.81'	Map 5
Cedar Point Light	N38° 18.24'	W76° 21.45'	Map 5
Cedar Point Hollow	N38° 15.54'	W76° 21.96'	Map 5
Buoy 72	N38° 15.40'	W76° 15.75'	Map 5
Targets	N38° 13.05'	W76° 18.94'	Map 5
HS Buoy	N38° 12.31'	W76° 14.53'	Map 5
Richland Light	N38° 12.40'	W76° 09.32'	Map 5
Fish Hawk	N38° 08.94'	W76° 17.73'	Map 5
SW Middle Grounds	N38° 00.59'	W76° 10.98'	Map 5
Mud Leads	N38° 00.78'	W76° 06.86'	Map 5

Gary James of North Point Yacht Club with a nice spring rockfish
caught trolling off of Bloody Point Light

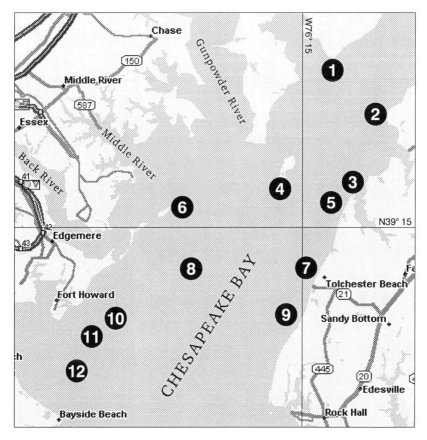

MAP 1 - UPPER BAY - Abbey Point to 7 Foot Knoll

1 — Abbey Point . . . . N39° 19.93' . . . W76° 12.57'

2 Worton Point . . . . N39° 19.44' . . . W76° 11.55'

3 — Handys Bar . . . . N39° 17.18' . . . W76° 13.01'

4 Pooles Island . . . . N39° 16.09' . . . W76° 15.71'

5 — Shallow Shoal . . . . N39° 16.42' . . . W76° 14.61'

6 Miller Island . . . . N39° 15.15' . . . W76° 19.67'

7 — Tolchester . . . . N39° 12.86' . . . W76° 14.90'

8 Sparty's Lump . . . . N39° 12.67' . . . W76° 19.17'

9 — Hodge's Bar . . . . N39° 11.24' . . . W76° 16.41'

10 Man of War Shoal . . . . N39° 11.18' . . . W76° 21.98'

11 — Craig Hill Light . . . . N39° 11.16' . . . W76° 23.93'

12 7 Foot Knoll . . . . N39° 09.30' . . . W76° 24.50'

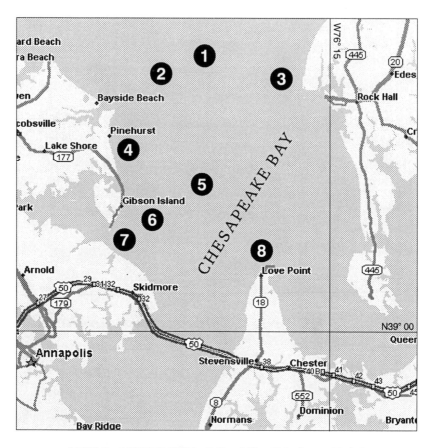

MAP 2 - UPPER BAY - 9 Foot Knoll to Love Point

1 — 9 Foot Knoll . . . . N39° 08.75' . . . W76° 21.87'

2 — 6 Foot Knoll . . . . N39° 08.62' . . . W76° 21.89'

3 — Swan Point . . . . N39° 07.86' . . . W76° 19.14'

4 — Snake Reef . . . . N39° 06.61' . . . W78° 25.50'

5 — Belvedere Shoal . . . . . N39° 06.00' . . . W76° 22.01'

6 — Baltimore Light . . . . . . N39° 03.50' . . . W76° 23.90'

7 — Podickery Point . . . . . . N39° 02.10' . . . W76° 24.01'

8 — Love Point . . . . N39° 03.47' . . . W76° 19.42'

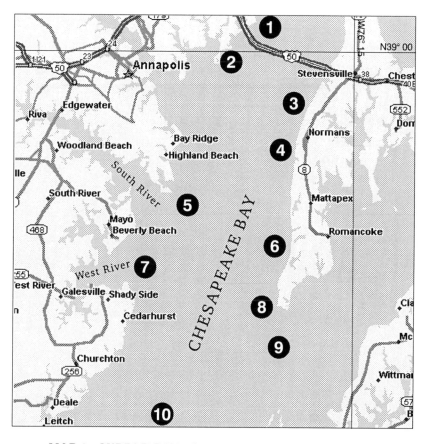

MAP 3 - MIDDLE BAY - Sandy Point Light to Buoy #83

1 — Sandy Point Light .... N39° 01.01' ... W76° 23.12'

2 Hackett's Bar........ N38° 58.18' ... W76° 25.09'

3 — Matapeake.......... N38° 57.64' ... W76° 21.89'

4 Kentmoor Marina..... N38° 54.92' ... W76° 22.29'

5 — Thomas Point Light... N38° 54.01' ... W76° 25.83'

6 Gum Thickets .... N38° 52.52' ... W76° 23.22'

7 — Green Flasher .... N38° 51.87' ... W76° 27.02'

8 Bloody Point Light.... N38° 50.24' ... W76° 23.95'

9 — The Hill .... N38° 46.85' ... W76° 23.82'

10 Buoy #83 .... N38° 45.09' ... W76° 26.85'

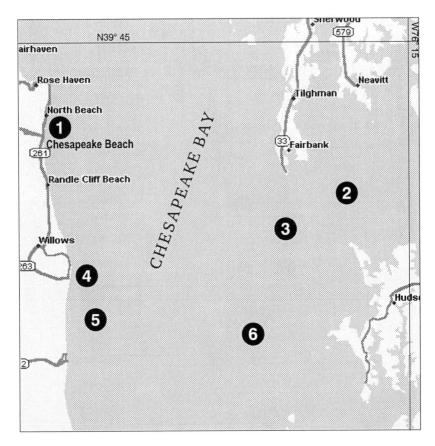

MAP 4 - MIDDLE BAY - Chesapeake Beach to Summer Gooses

1 — Chesapeake Beach. . . N38° 41.58' . . . W76° 31.40'

2 — Airplane Wreck . . . . . . N38° 39.60' . . . W76° 16.01'

3 — Sharp Island Light . . . . N38° 39.51' . . . W76° 22.62'

4 — Breezy Point . . . . N38° 36.94' . . . W76° 30.70'

5 — Clancy's . . . . N38° 34.67' . . . W76° 29.41

6 — Summer Gooses . . . . . N38° 31.61' . . . W76° 23.02'

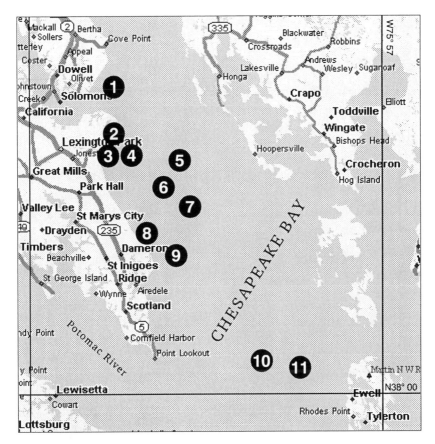

MAP 5 - LOWER BAY - Solomons Island to Maryland Line

1 — Chinese Mud . . . . N38° 19.54' . . . W76° 22.64'

2 — Cedar Point . . . . N38° 18.79' . . . W76° 22.81'

3 — Cedar Point Light . . . . N38° 18.24' . . . W76° 21.45'

4 — Cedar Point Hollow . . . N38° 15.54' . . . W76° 21.96'

5 — Buoy 72 . . . . N38° 15.40' . . . W76° 15.75'

6 — Targets . . . . N38° 13.05' . . . W76° 18.94'

7 — HS Buoy . . . . N38° 12.31' . . . W76° 14.53'

8 — Richland Light . . . . N38° 12.40' . . . W76° 09.32'

9 — Fish Hawk . . . . N38° 08.94' . . . W76° 17.73'

10 — SW Middle Grounds . . N38° 00.59' . . . W76° 10.98'

11 — Mud Leads. . . . . N38° 00.78' . . . W76° 06.86'

Ed Kraemer fishing on the *"Oh Thank Heaven"* at Bloody Point

 # FISHING ETHICS & COURTESY

Before the start of another fishing season, I would like to take this opportunity to discuss some problems that you should try to avoid during the season.

While most fishermen know that good fishing ethics are important, there are quite a few anglers who show little courtesy while fishing on the bay.

First, let's talk about chumming. When you are approaching several boats that are anchored and engaged in fishing, please approach these boats slowly and not from their sterns. These boats could be chumming and are creating a chum line behind their boats. It is important and only a matter of courtesy to alter your course and not drive your boat through their chum line. If you wish to fish the area, please anchor your boat to either side of the boats anchored or in front (up-tide) of the boats. Be sure that your anchor is set before you start to fish. There is nothing more frustrating, after you have established your chum line, for a boat to drag his anchor through it. If you wish to anchor below (down-tide) these boats, please allow a large buffer zone, so as not to throw your anchor in their established chum line. Never troll or drift fish through these boats or directly behind their sterns. This is very unethical and could provoke the serious fisherman to throw a few sinkers at your boat. This same set of fishing ethics apply to an anchored boat that is bottom fishing.

Trolling brings a different set of ethics. Try to conform to the trolling pattern that has been established by a group of boats. If it is a north/south pattern, don't try to go east/west. Several times, especially in the Upper Bay, a trolling pattern may have you going over a particular lump against the tide. After you have passed the spot, bring in your lines and proceed slowly (no wake) back to the lump and fall in line when it is your turn.

While trolling try to make wide turns and stay well ahead of a boat that may be on your port or starboard. Never cut in front of another boat while you are trolling. This could cost you to lose several lines. If you observe a boat that is catching a fish, give him as much leeway as possible. The captain may have to steer to port or starboard in order to control the fish or to keep his lines from tangling.

Another issue to be aware of is the use of planer boards. Pay attention while trolling among other boats. Planer boards have become more popular each year. Watch out for these boards which could be as much as a couple of hundred feet away from the boat. If you observe these boards, please give them a wide berth, you don't want to get tangled with them.

These are only a few fishing ethics that we should be aware of and practice. Most of these fishing ethics and courteous practices have a lot to do with using your common sense. Let's hope that these fishing ethics will be observed throughout the entire fishing season.

My Dad, showing my Brother, Ron, how big his fish was

 # FISHERMEN'S KNOTS

Probably the most agonizing task to learn in fishing is tying knots correctly. The ability to tie proper fishing knots is the most critical factor in fishing. It means landing that big fish of a lifetime or looking at a curly pig tail at the end of your line. Knots are the weakest link of your fishing equipment.

In learning how to tie knots correctly, practice tying with a heavy monofilament line material, cord or small diameter rope. Be sure to only tie your knot with the recommended twist or turns. Additional or less twists or turns will reduce the integrity of the knot. Tie your knot properly, then slowly tighten up your knot as tight as possible, then cut off your tag end within an eighth of an inch of the knot.

BLOOD KNOT

1.   Cross the two lines and wrap each line three
     times around the other.

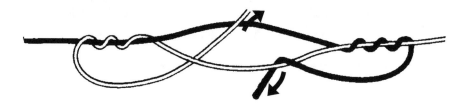

2.   Take the tag end of each line and bring it back
     through it's loop in the center.

3.   Pull on both ends of your running line until the
     lines tighten.

SNELLING A HOOK

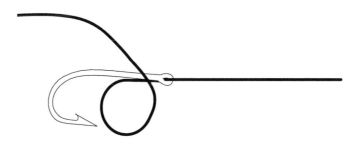

1. Place your leader line through the eye of the
    hook and leave about 6 inches of line
    remaining. Now form a loop.

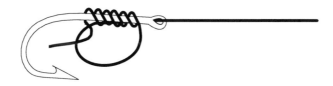

2. Work towards the point and wrap six turns
    through the loop and around the shank of the
    hook.

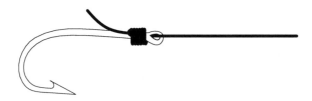

3. Pull you leader line tight to finish the knot.
    Cut off remaining tag end.

IMPROVED CLINCH KNOT

1. Pass the line end through the eye of the hook. Leave about six inches of line remaining through the hook.

2. Hold the hook in one hand and wrap the tag end five times around your running line. Now pass the line end back through the first loop at the eye, then back into the loop that you just formed.

3. Pull running line tight and cut off tag end.

PALOMAR KNOT

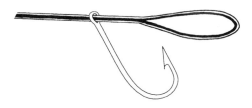

1. Double about six inches of line and pass the loop through the eye of the hook.

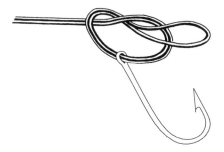

2. Take the loop back and tie an overhand knot.

3. Take the loop around the hook.

4. Pull the standing line to tighten the knot and snip off tag end.

SPIDER HITCH

1.   Double your line and then make a loop in it.

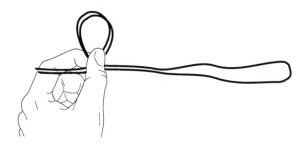

2.   Hold the loop tight with your thumb and forefinger.

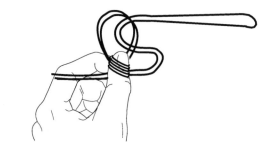

3.   Wrap the double line five times around your thumb and insert the end through the original loop.

4.   Slowly pull the loops off your thumb and tighten knot.

DROPPER LOOP

1. Make a loop in line and begin turning eight to
    ten times around the line.

2. Pull loop through center opening.

3. Hold loop in teeth and tighten.

NON-SLIP MONO LOOP

1. Tie overhand knot six to eight inches up from
    leader. Insert through eye of leader, then back
    through loop in knot.

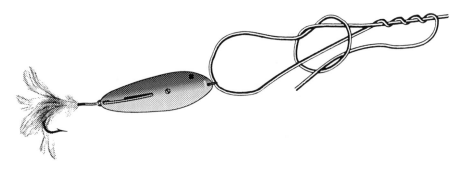

2. Wrap line three to four times around line, then back
    through loop.

3. Pull line end to tighten knot, then pull main line.

BERKLEY TRILENE KNOT

1. Pull line through eye of hook two times.

2. Wrap around line three times and pull back through the two loops.

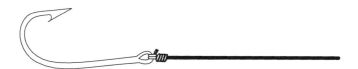

3. Pull line to tighten.

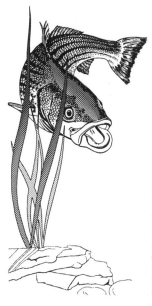

My Dad proudly displaying his trophy bass

 # MARK THAT SPOT

It was the last day of the striped bass recreational fishing season in Maryland. October 26th came in as one of the foggiest days in 1991. I met my dad and several other friends at a local restaurant at 6:00 a.m. By 6:40 a.m. we had finished our breakfast and were on our way down to the boatyard.

Upon arriving at the boat, each member of my crew did their assigned tasks before we got underway. Dad was in charge of wiping off the windows inside and out. Danny and Jimmy stored all of the crews ice chests and bags inside the cabin so they would be out of the way while fishing. Dave pulled the live box aboard and dumped two dozen eels into a five gallon bucket and iced them down. I was busy mounting my electronics (radio, depth finder and loran) into position. Roger was putting the spinning rods into the rod holders in the transom of the boat - as we pulled away from the pier.

My crew did an outstanding job and we were on our way by 7:10. This day was no different than the last three previous days as we were greeted by a fog bank within a quarter mile of the pier - or so we thought! As we made our way through the fog it became more intense and visibility was down to 50 feet.

 I entered my first waypoint number into my loran to guide me through the fog. I kept a very close eye on my compass and then on my loran to keep a true course. After reaching my first waypoint, I entered waypoint number 3 into my loran to guide me for the next 2.7 miles. Somehow we were able to reach our destination without hitting another boat or object in the water. Now I entered waypoint number 34 in my loran and proceeded on a heading of 175 degrees toward Swan Point. Each member of my crew kept a watchful eye as we proceeded across the bay to Swan Point. As we neared our fishing location, the crew became very alert to our surroundings because we were nearing the shipping channel. Since we were still in a heavy fog and visibility was only 100 feet at best, you can't imagine the images and sounds that are created in your mind as we crossed the shipping channel. I guess God was with us because we did arrive at our destination safely.

It was now 8:50 as we started baiting our lines with the live eels. Since we iced down our eels before leaving, we were able to handle the slippery critters pretty easily with a dry towel. As we impaled them on  our hooks and slipped them into the warm waters of the bay, they came to life and started swimming frantically After twenty minutes of riding around we located a school of fish to drop our eels on. As I stopped the forward motion of the boat, by reversing my engines - and before I had a chance to say "*drop 'em*" - my Dad who always "*jumps the gun*" - already had his eel on the bottom. A minute later my Dad hollered "*fish on*" and the fight was on. We were using fairly light tackle - 6 foot medium spinning rods and Shimano AX300 reels loaded with 14 pound test line. As I reached for the net on the side of my boat, I noticed that Danny had set his hook on another Rockfish. Within a couple of minutes my Dad had his fish to the boat. I lowered the net into the water and Dad brought the fish to it - with one swoop of the net the fish became a statistic. I didn't waste anytime getting the fish out of the net because Danny was hollering for me to net his fish. I quickly dumped the fish onto the deck and quickly raced to net Danny's fish. By the time I had Danny's fish on the deck, my Dad had already removed his hook and was putting his striped bass tag into the mouth of the fish. Through the course of the season I found that this was the best method to tag the fish. Earlier we were placing a piece of monofilament in the fish's mouth and out through the gill and tied on the tag. By the end of the day, several tags were laying in the water at the bottom of the fish box and not on the fish. During those first few years after the moratorium, anglers were issued tags to be used during the season. Use all your tags and your season was ended.

I quickly got behind the wheel and informed my crew to pull in their lines so that we could make another drift. I did manage to throw out a marker after the first fish was hooked. We had to be very careful not to drift far from our marker since the visibility was only about 100 feet. As I proceeded back to my marker - about five other boats were charging toward the spot.

That's eel fishing in the Upper Bay! As soon as you wave the net or throw a marker all eyes are on you and shortly thereafter you are surrounded by boats. After reaching the spot, I waited for the other boats to position themselves to make their drift. Two out of the five boats hooked up as they passed my marker. The other three captains went on the wrong side of the marker - missing the fish. We were now in line to make our drift. It was perfect! Dave was first to yell "*fish on*". followed by Jimmy and Danny again. Roger also was hooked up but lost his fish after a short battle. As we completed our drift we were able to net all three fish and they went into box.

As I started back to the "*hot spot*" I noticed that the visibility was getting better and more boats were approaching. By this time a dozen or so boats were in the area. Again as we drifted toward our jug, I felt a hard tug on my line, followed by two others and my line started to pull toward the other side of the boat. I set the hook with a hard yank and the fight began. I was the only one to get a hook-up on that pass but what a thrill it was! As Dave netted the fish for me, I noticed the hook was barely set in the lower jaw of the fish and as soon as the fish hit the deck, the fish spit the 6/0 hook.

We were able to make three more drifts and caught one more fish before there were so many boats on the spot that the fish scattered. Within a half hour the tide stopped and we started looking for other areas to fish. We went to several other places but we were never able to attract another fish to take our eels.

The fog never did lift and by late afternoon it was starting to roll back in. We decided to call it a day since we had seven nice fish in the box measuring from 28 to 33-1/2 inches. All of us did not get a chance to use our tags on this last day of the season - but everyone felt that it was great to be able to fish for rockfish - once again!

FALL STRIPED BASS SEASON 1991

On Thursday November 14th, the Department of Natural Resources made the announcement "*the recreational Striped Bass season would be extended for the following weekend*", which was November 16th and November 17th. This was the news that I had been waiting to hear all week. I was sure that we would have this weekend to pursue our favorite pastime "*Catching Rockfish*" since the previous weekend was a bust with winds gusting to 40 knots.

All I had to do was to make a few phone calls to my friends that I had already lined up in the beginning of the week, and tell them what time to meet me at the boat. I usually fish out of Middle River during the Striped Bass Fishery but since it was getting later in the year, I knew that the fish would be on the move southward. I moved my boat down the bay to Kentmoor Marina, which is approximately 5 miles below the Bay Bridge. This would give me the advantage to fish the 'Winter Hole" which is just above the Bay Bridge or we could head South and fish Gum Thickets and Eastern Bay.

During the previous week, I fished on Friday before the wind came through for the weekend. I was able to limit out with 10 nice stripers ranging from 28 inches to 33 inches. I fished Eastern Bay and was back at the dock within three hours.

On this weekend, my game plan was to fish southwards toward Bloody Point Light and end up in Eastern Bay - if I didn't catch anything along Kent Island. I started looking for fish near Buoy #86 - which is just off Gum Thickets. I usually don't start fishing an area until I see fish on my depth finder. I moved southward toward Bloody Point Light but I never did see any concentration of fish to make me stop and fish. I then headed toward Eastern Bay. Several of my friends were fishing near the #1 marker which is located just inside the mouth of Eastern Bay. They called me on the radio to say that there had been a few fish caught and it looked like they were getting ready to bite. That was all I needed to hear! I pushed the throttles forward and was in Eastern Bay in five minutes.

As soon as we got into Eastern Bay in approximately 45 feet of water, I had my crew drop their lines in the water. With just three minutes of trolling, Ed hollered "fish on" and the fight began. A few minutes later Ed landed a 31 inch rockfish. As I turned the boat to go back to the spot where we hooked up, Howard yelled "fish on" followed by Frank - stating the same. Two more fish went into the box one 26 inches long and the other was 28 inches. By 2:00 the wind started to pick up and we decided to return to Kentmoor with our catch. We caught over 30 rockfish out of which 10 nice size keepers were in our fish-box, with the smallest one being 26 inches and the largest being 33 inches. Every fish that was caught was well over the minimum size limit of 18 inches.

The weather was perfect with light winds and temperatures climbing to 65 degrees by mid-day. Several other boats were in the immediate area, but everyone was courteous and each of us "gave way" when approaching another boat. Several MSSA members were

fishing the area and were heard on the VHF
radios stating when they had a hook-up, to
help each other locate the fish.

On Sunday I had to talk my crew into going
since the winds were from the North at 20
miles per hour. I told them that we had a good
day yesterday and we would be in the lee of
the wind in Eastern Bay. The marine radio said
the winds would calm down by noon, so we
left the marina and headed to Eastern Bay. Again fishing was great and
the bay became like a sheet of glass by mid-day. Before leaving for
home-port we had caught 22 rockfish for the day and had 12 fish that
were over 30 inches in the box, with the largest being 35-1/2 inches.

One of the reasons for writing this story is to let other fishermen
know that there are plenty of fish still available in late Fall - if you use
the proper techniques. I would like to share with you the method I
used to rig my trolling lines. Start with a basic bottom bouncing
trolling rig with an 18 foot
leader. Use a 16 to 20 ounce
weight to get the lines near the
bottom - since we were fishing in
40 to 70 feet of water.

Luckily, several other captains
were in the area and told me
that they were catching large
rockfish. They noticed that they
were feeding on large baitfish
(alewives) that were still in the
area. Usually this time of year
the rockfish are feeding on
silversides, bay anchovies or
minnows because the large
baitfish have departed by this
time. As usual, you always want
to match the size lure to the size
baitfish that are in the area.

With all of this in mind, I took off my traditional 1/0 to 3/0 bucktails and attached 7/0 to 9/0 bucktails. I dressed each one of my bucktails with long plastic split-tails to enhance their movement through the water. On several other lines, I attached 9/0 Crippled Alewive. I used several different colors and they all caught fish but the hottest line was a green and yellow 9/0 Crippled Alewive. I couldn't believe what was happening. These are the baits that I usually pull during the spring-time, and not late fall. Like any good fisherman, you must change your tactics when conditions change in a particular season or year. This was the case! Since there were still large baitfish in the area, it only made sense to use larger lures.

One other thing I noticed with using the larger lures was that I was catching a size fish that was well beyond the minimum size limit. Every fish that I caught was large enough to keep. I noticed other boats in the area and what baits they were using. I saw several boats releasing smaller fish that were well below the 18 inch minimum size - due to that fact that they were using smaller lures. It occurred to me that because of using larger lures, I was actually culling my catch before they came overboard. You can be sure that I will try this same tactic for the next Striped Bass Season!

 # FISH THE BIRDS

It was October 24th, 1992 and the winds had finally settled down from 15 mph the day before to light and variable. I met my party at the local McDonald's for breakfast at 6:30 a.m. and by 7 we were onboard the "*Oh Thank Heaven*". I knew that the party wanted to do some light tackle fishing, so I pulled up my homemade "*live box*", a five gallon bucket filled with holes floating on the water and dumped out two dozen eels into another five gallon bucket that I had onboard. I immediately proceeded to fill the bucket with ice to help settle down the lively eels. Usually within a half hour, eels become lethargic and are easier to handle. You still must use a dry rag or paper towel to hand on to those slippery devils. Even though I had stopped fishing with eels for a week or so, I thought that if I saw a good concentration of fish on my depth finder I would give eel fishing another try.

My game plan was to go through the Pleasure Island Channel in order to check out a few spots on the way, in case a few birds may be working the area. Just off of Rocky Point I spotted a few birds working in Hawkes Cove. Although there were less than 20 birds working I wanted to try the spot anyway. I brought out the spinning tackle that was already rigged with 5/0 bucktails and 4 inch sassy shads. One member of the party, Tony, brought his fly rod so I instructed him to fish off the bow of the boat so that he could cast freely. Several small fish from 12 to 20 inches were caught over the next 20 minutes, but I did manage to put a 26 inch rockfish in the box. I knew because of fishing in the area for the last several days that there should be more birds working on the other side of the islands. I got Tony off of the bow and we proceeded out into the Bay. We were heading toward an area between Fort Howard and 7 Foot Knoll.

I gave up eel fishing on the 15th of the month and started trolling for rockfish. Eel fishing was very productive up until that time but due to foul weather and winds constantly blowing from 15 to 25 mph it was very hard to find the fish in the areas that we were working. I was mainly working from Pooles Island to the Middle Lump located just a few miles southeast from the Hart-Miller Island Dike. On the way to whatever area I was going to work that day I usually saw birds working over breaking fish. On several occasions I stopped for 15 to 20 minutes to check out the "grade" of fish that the birds were working over. Most of the time they were 10 to 18 inches especially if they were in shallow water or on top of the shoals.

I had been working the mouth of the Patapsco River for the past three days and had limited out each day. I saw plenty of birds working during those trips so I thought that I would begin in that area. I knew that if we could not catch a good grade of fish by casting over working birds that we would be close to the area by which we could troll and catch 24 to 30 inch fish. As soon as I came out from the

Pleasure Island Channel and headed south, I saw several flocks of birds working the water. Within 10 minutes we were on the birds and my party was casting to them. Tony gave up on his fly rod and switched over to his light spinning tackle outfit that he had brought with him.

The action lasted all morning until the tide stopped. By this time we had almost reached our quotas with fish ranging from 24 to 28 inches. Since the birds stopped working during the slack tide everyone took advantage of the lull and ate their lunch. We were ready to fish when the tide started to turn a half hour later. We would work the area where the birds were flying until we saw another heavy concentration of birds working. Although the birds may fly off a particular spot does not mean that the fish have left. Simply cast your bucktail to where the birds were and let it sink to the bottom. Slowly work your bucktail back across the bottom and quite often you will have a pick up. A good idea is to watch your depth finder while working over breaking fish. Quite often you will see a large concentration of fish on or near the bottom. Let your lure sink to the bottom before retrieving it. We did this on several occasions and improved the size of fish that we were catching near the surface.

By 3 o'clock we had reached our limit and were heading back to port. Because we were using artificial lures and not live bait we were able to release over 100 fish unharmed. 99 times out of 100 these fish were lip hooked and it was very easy to remove the lure and release the fish unharmed. If you are planning to try this type of fishing next season, one suggestion is to use a pair of pliers to flatten down the barb in order to make releasing fish easier. Fishing a barb-less hook will not reduce the number of fish caught but will help in releasing them harmlessly. In fact, the Chesapeake Bay Foundation and the Department of Natural Resources have developed the *"Careful Catch Program"* promoting fishing with barb-less hooks.

Remember to take your spinning tackle during the striped bass season for 1993. Look for the birds and more importantly - have fun.

 # REMINISCING THE '93 SEASON

As I sit here gazing out the window watching the ground being covered with a blanket of snow, my thoughts take me back to the fall rockfish season. Oh! What a season it was!

The 1993 striped bass season was a very memorable one, full of joy, excitement, and disappointment. Joy came on opening day when I was able to conclude my second rockfishing trip by 12:00 noon. This was the only day that I had two trips scheduled. I met my first party at a local McDonalds at 6:00 a.m. Breakfast was a couple of egg and biscuit sandwiches and a cup of 7-11 coffee that I brought with me. By 6:20 my party and I were on the highway heading toward my marina which was three miles away. Since the opening of the striped bass season I have always scheduled that day for my friends and my Dad. Included in the party besides my Dad, was my brother-in-law, Bill and four MSSA members. Conditions were ideal with light winds, 50 degree temperature, and calm water. From past experiences, I knew that I did not have to go far to fish for rockfish on opening day. A three mile ride out of Middle River and I was at the "*Dike*". This was to be my first spot. Upon arriving, a "*pack*" of boats were already on the spot, probably 50 to 75 boats. A quick call on the radio to someone I recognized in the crowd, informed me that the bite was good just before sunrise and lasted for 30 minutes. He said that there were still a few being caught but the action had really slowed down. With this piece of information, I kept the boat heading Southeast. I knew that a better concentration of fish should be located near Gales Lumps, 3.5 miles outside the Hart-Miller Island Complex. I could see on the horizon that another collection of boats were near that location. By the time we reached the *"hot spot"* there were 50 or more boats drifting. Slowing down, I told my Dad to break out the spinning rods. They were already rigged for eel fishing. Everyone grabbed a rod and reached into the ice bucket and hooked on a live eel. After riding around for a few minutes, I located a concentration of fish on my depth finder which were on a small lump. I quickly circled and slowed the boat until I was over the fish and reversed my engines to stop the boat. I told the crew to "*drop those eels*". It only took 30 seconds before we had two pickups and were bringing a couple of rockfish into the boat. As I netted the second fish I looked up to see a dozen boats approaching me at full speed. Once a net is waved in the air it is like dropping the flag at the Indianapolis 500. I quickly got behind the helm and proceeded back to the same spot. As I jockeyed for a position among the boats, I saw the fish on the depth finder again telling my crew to drop their eels. Four rods went down almost simultaneously. These were a nice grade of fish. The fish were in the 28 to 32 inch size range thus making it very difficult to try to horse the fish while using light tackle. Six and half foot, medium spinning rods with Shimano 300 spinning reels were a perfect combination to feel the thrill of the fight. Two more passes and we limited out for the day.

Twelve nice striped bass were in the cooler. The second trip was right back to the same location and within an hour we had the same results.

Disappointment came all too soon. In fact, it was the very next day. Winds blowing out of the northwest at 20 to 25 knots. Fishing in the open part of the Bay was impossible with four to five foot seas. My party still wanted to get the day of fishing  in. Trying to make the best out of the situation, I went inside the Patapsco River seeking some relief from the weather. Eight hours later we managed to catch two rockfish of legal size 26 and 29 inches, before returning to home port.

Sunday, the third day of the season, was a perfect morning with light winds. I headed straight out to Gales Lumps and was greeted by an armada of 100 boats or more. Boat sizes ranged from 12 foot jon boats to 50 foot Hatteras. On the way out to the spot I checked several crab pot floats and noticed that they were lying still in the water, which meant that we were having a slack tide. It was now a waiting game until the tide started to move. An hour later the tide started to ebb and the fish started to bite! Boat traffic became so hectic that I had just enough time to net an incoming fish and get back to my helm before colliding with another boat. It was like bumper cars! Holding your fishing rod in hand and pushing off a boat with the other. Fortunately, by 11:00 a.m. we limited out just before another front came through with 20+ knot winds.

The remainder of the month of October was very stressful for most upper bay captains. One day you would limit out with a nice catch of stripes, return to the same location the next day and be lucky to pull out two or three fish. October of '93 saw more windy days than calm ones. The problems associated with these windy days are that they disturb the normal flow of the tides. Many days had only one tide change and eight to ten hours of slack tide. If you ask any *"old salt"* he'll tell you without a tide you're not going to catch rockfish.

Water temperatures remained warm for the entire month of October, in the 60 degree range. Rockfish generally don't school until the water temperatures are in the mid to low 50's range. This did not happen until mid-November. By this time the season was winding down. Most anglers were beginning to pull their boats for winter storage. As the final week of fishing in November approached, there were not longer armadas of boats to look for. Most boats were scattered with just a few small clusters working over a pod of fish. Those who were willing to brave the wind and cold were treated to some fantastic fishing trips. In fact, the average size of striper increased with many coming cross the transom over the previous year maximum limit of 36 inches.

Did I mention about the breaking fish during the final month of the season? Birds were working over these fish all day long. From the upper bay to Point Lookout, birds could be seen working. The only problem was the size of these breaking fish was 12 to 17 inches in the upper bay. Every once in a while you caught one of legal size, 18 inches. The average was I out of 20, if you were lucky. I was trolling large baits, 8/0 to 10/0 bucktails, 6 inch sassy shads, 9/0 Crippled Alewives, and 4 oz. parachutes. Due to the size of my lures I never even had to pull while going through these breaking fish. Needless to say, I didn't bother trying to fish for these smaller fish after the first few tries. We were after a much better grade (size) of rockfish.

The '93 striped bass season was at times frustrating, seeing fish on the depth finder and not being able to catch them. Of course there were many more days that were exciting, full of laughter, telling of jokes, anticipating strikes all while trying to catch your quota of rockfish. Yes, the '93 season still turned out to be a great one!

 # QUEST FOR A TROPHY

The winter of '97 has to go into the history books as being one of the warmest winters, temperature-wise, for several decades. Due to those mild days, many of our fisheries should start much earlier than usual.

Yellow perch are now being caught in their usual haunts as the calendar slips into March. Buds can be seen on trees as they are preparing to blossom into their magnificent colors.

The last sport show concluded in Solomons Island on March 23rd. By this time everyone should have a good dose of cabin fever. Only one more month and anglers will be able to put their lines in the water to capture that elusive trophy striped bass.

One must remember why these monster bass are in our Chesapeake Bay at this time of year. They are here to do what their parents and grandparents have done for the last several centuries - spawn! This is truly one part of their life cycle that they must accomplish every year. Scientists have proven that these magnificent creatures come back year after year, not just to the Chesapeake Bay but to the very river systems where they were first given life.

Just think of it, these gentle beauties have survived thousands of miles of gill nets that try to capture them every year from Maine to North Carolina. How can they possibly maneuver their way up and down the Coast without getting entangled in the many kinds of nets trying to capture them? Better yet, how can they remain free off the coast of North Carolina when there are no less than four different kinds of net fisheries pursuing them?

If these majestic swimmers are able to meet their rendezvous with destiny and spawn in the Chesapeake Bay, they then must prepare for the havoc that will plague them by the recreational angler. Lures that imitate bait fish that these line-siders feed upon are pulled or cast through the water. Spoons, such as Crippled Alewives, Tony Acetta's, and Huntington Drones are awaiting them with a variety of shapes and colors. Bucktails and parachutes or other plugs like the Stretch 25 or Rat-L Traps will try to lure them into biting. Ah, but these giants did not get to be 50 or 60 pounds by falling for a metal fish dragged behind a boat. You may be able to coax a juvenile of 20 to 30 pounds but outsmarting an adult with broad shoulders and better than 55 inches in length will test your skills and endurance.

Yes, these wise old fish have seen all the tricks but maybe, yes maybe, you just might catch her a little off guard one day. Her eyesight may be getting a bit more blurred with age. She knows that with each passing year she is not as quick as she once was pursuing menhaden on the Atlantic. Her tail was shortened by two inches due to her last encounter with a shark cruisin' off Martha's Vineyard this past summer. The rigors of spawning have taken a lot out of her and she is looking for an easy meal. Could it be, could it be that she's ready to grab your lure and you're ready to take on the battle of your lifetime. After the initial hit and you have fought her for 20 minutes, which seems like hours now, are you thinking about your leader line? Is it of high quality or did you purchase it at a discount outlet and really don't know how long it has been on the shelf? Did you tie those knots properly and are you sure your swivels were properly closed? All of these things cross your mind while doing battle with this 50 pound monster. Since gaffs aren't allowed to be used in Maryland while striper fishing, how big is your net? Better still, who is going to leader the fish in and who is going to be on the net? Here is where more fish are lost than swung over the side.

Are you now possessed like Captain Ahab was in "*Moby Dick*" in capturing your prey? Do you see her behind the boat as she angrily arcs her back and exposes her dorsal fin? Do you see that broad tail slashing back and forth to obtain some advantage in producing slack in the line? Do you see her opening her huge mouth and your lure is dangling from its side? Did your crew  clear all of the other lines and stow them so as not to become entangled? Do you feel the tremendous pull on the leader line as you try to gain a few inches with each handful? Does she pull the leader back through your hands as she makes another run from your boat? Do you have gloves on or did the leader just slice a groove in the palm of your hand and your forefinger? How long has it been, 25-30-40-50 minutes, since she first took your offering?

All of these questions go through your mind as you are battling that trophy fish. Then the big moment comes when you bring the net back over the side with 50 pounds of rockfish. Jubilation goes through the entire crew as they glare at this magnificent beauty. "*High Fives*" are exchanged as you watch the lure become dislodged with one final shake of the head.

During the remainder of the day your crew keeps opening the fish-box as if somehow the fish could have escaped or do they just want to admire its beauty! Are you having second thoughts about keeping the fish? Should you have let her go even though you could tell that she had already spawned? Even if you would have let her go, would she have been able to survive after expending all of her energy during the battle? Probably not?

This is your day! Enjoy it and be sure to take plenty of pictures for future memories, so you will always remember.

Casi Favre, while visiting from Florida, captured this beauty

 # WHAT A FISHERY!

It was like someone turning on a switch that started the second season of Maryland's striped bass fishery. On June 15th the size limit for rockfish was reduced to 18 inches with a two fish creel. Rockfish showed up everywhere overnight! It was like they knew that it was time to come out of the river systems and into the Bay.

From the mouth of Chester River to the Potomac, rockfish were everywhere. It didn't matter what method you used to catch them; they all worked. Trollers worked the Upper Bay from Baltimore Light to Sandy Point Light and limited out in a couple of hours. From the Bay Bridge south, chummers were reaching their limits in an hour or two and were hoisting their anchors to locate other species such as white perch, hardheads. trout and flounder. In addition, jigging or casting artificial lures in the shallows, piers, bridges, shoreline and other visible structure produced nice catches of rockfish.

What was so surprising during this fishery was the size of the stripers. Yes, we had the expected 16 to 22 inch range that has been the norm for the past couple of seasons. But this year we had an unusual amount of 30 inch plus fish. During the course of a full day fishing trip, you were rewarded with maybe two to six rockfish over the 30 inch mark. This phenomenon held up pretty consistently in the Upper to Mid-Bay. Anglers fishing from Solomons to the Potomac enjoyed consistent creel limits of 28 to 33 inches.

Another surprising observation was the very small numbers of dead rockfish floating on the surface. In the past couple of years it would not be unusual to count up to 20 to 30 rockfish floating by your boat while you were anchored chumming. I think this is to the credit of the DNR. For the past two years they have been promoting the use of circle hooks while chumming for rockfish.

Please let me preach to you one more time on the use of circle hooks. Try them! But you must use them exclusively or you must know and keep track of which rods have circle hooks. Leave them in the rod holders and let them catch the fish for you. Circle hooks are your future. Try not to be so hardheaded like I was until two years ago, After hearing from other fishermen and other charter-boat captains on how effective they were in reducing mortality I forced myself to learn to use them. Now I think these hooks are the greatest things since sliced bread in protecting and preserving our striped bass fishery. If you won't do it for yourself, than do it for your children and grandchildren.

 # FISHING OUT OF KENTMOOR

Weather forecasters on the TV predicted 5 to 10 mph winds out of the northwest for tomorrow's weather. I called five of my fishing buddies and they all agreed to go fishing the next day.

I went downstairs to check my freezer in my basement. After a quick inventory I decided that I had enough chum and bait for tomorrow's trip. Before hitting the sack at 9:00 p.m. I set the alarm clock for 3:00 a.m. As soon as it went off I got up, dressed and drove the truck to the back of the house in order to get the chum and bait from the cellar. Loading it in the truck I was off to the Double T Diner for breakfast. Ham and eggs and two cups of coffee and I was off again.

It's now 5:00 a.m., and I've got to stop at Angler's Sport Shop to buy block ice. After talking to several of the clerks on where the fish are biting, I was off again. Crossing the Bay Bridge I took the first exit south on Route 8 to the Shore Shop for another cup of coffee to go and finally arrived at my boat by 5:30 a.m.

My crew showed up precisely at the scheduled time of 6:15 a.m. They stowed their gear below, untied the lines, and we were pulling out of the slip by 6:30. A half-hour ride north brought us to Love Point. As I set the anchor the crew was busy getting the rods out of the cabin and clearing the fish box of the cutting board, measuring box and portable rod holders. The anchor caught on the first attempt as I laid out additional scope.

We hung the chum bucket off the port cleat and within a minute we had a chum slick behind the boat. We then cut up three or four frozen alewives as bait. We punctured each piece of bait so the circle hook was easier to put on the hook. We baited the eleven rods and waited for our first strike. It didn't take long. Within three minutes, Jim was battling a rockfish that hit one of the floater lines. Dan grabbed the net and swooped the striper out of the water. He then placed the fish on the measuring board and called out 35-1/2 inches. WOW! What a way to start the day. Before we could get the rockfish into the fish box, another rod went off. By the time Bud got to the port-side rod it was bent in half and line was stripping off the reel. Dan was still holding onto the net so he netted this one as well. The fish was a keeper of 28 inches.

For the next hour we caught 11 more rockfish, however, only two of them were of legal size. By this time the tide slowed, so did the fishing or should I say catching. Shortly after the tide swung around, the fish started to bite. The side rods started the action off since these rods had 3 ounces of weight and were fished right on the bottom next to the boat. It was a real smorgasbord with 38, 32, 17 and 16-inch stripers, as well as two Atlantic croakers of 16 and 18-1/2 inches.

We were back to catching rockfish as the tide steadily picked up. It only took another hour for us to limit out with 12 beautiful rockfish from 18-1/2 inches to 38 inches. The secret to this successful trip was two-fold. I scoured the area to locate the fish on my depth finder before anchoring. I tried to anchor just above them so the tide would carry my chum and the baits back to them. Secondly, I keep the chum bucket just far enough in the water to keep a steady flow of chum going behind my boat.

By the time we were making our way back down the Bay the relatively calm seas were absolutely flat, like a sheet of glass. I was reflecting back on our trip while going back to the dock. I realized why we had such a great time and successful trip. Everyone shared in the responsibility of what was to be done during the course of the day. Bait had to be cut, additional chum had to be put into the chum bucket, lines had to be checked and re-baited often, someone had to net the larger fish, the gunnels and transom top had to be cleaned with the mop every few minutes. With everyone sharing in the responsibility, it made for a great fishing experience.

 # FISHING PARKER'S CREEK

It was another beautiful and pristine day on the Chesapeake Bay. A light, gentle breeze of five knots kissed your cheeks ever so softly. The sun broke the horizon and filled the clouds with red, orange, and yellow luminous. It had all the makings of a great fishing day on the most famous estuary in the world, the Chesapeake Bay.

Although I was scheduled to meet my fishing buddies at 6:30 on my boat, I arrived an hour earlier to make sure everything was in good shape. I brought out nine trolling rods that I was going to deploy for the day from the cabin. I checked to see that all of the lures (bucktails and parachutes) were cleaned from the last trip. I did have to hose off a couple of bucktails that were stained from the mahogany tide that had plagued us during the first several weeks of the striped bass season. I also loaded the boat down with plenty of ice for the coolers and for the fish box.

Dave was the first to arrive and knew to stow his gear and lunch box in the cabin. The remaining four arrived together since they drove down from Baltimore in one vehicle. Frank and Ron have fished with me on many occasions and knew the routine for casting off. Henry and John just sat back and let the younger members of the crew do the work. They did, however, offer a few comments on how the lines should be placed on the pier and the placement of the electrical line as we casted off.

It was 6:47 a.m. and we were out of the slip and on our way to the fishing grounds. I decided to fish the Parker Creek area since I learned that this was a "hot" location from the past several days. I heard reports of stripers over 30 inches and having a six angler crew limit out in two hours. The half-hour ride south was uneventful due to the flat calm seas.

I slowed the boat down approximately a mile from the Parker's Creek Can. I had Henry drive the boat as Frank and I played out the trolling lines. Meanwhile, Dave and Ron were getting out the dummy lines and leader line and John went in the cabin to get the umbrella rigs. It took us about 20 minutes to get all of the lines - nine rods and three dummy lines over board. When I finally got behind the wheel I saw that we were heading toward an armada of fishing boats. We were trolling the 32-foot contour line down to Parker's Creek. I observed several boats working close to shore in about 25 to 30 feet of water. However, I saw just as many boats working the deeper water of 35 to 45 feet. I could feel five pair of eyes burning into the back of my head wondering which way I was going to choose. I headed west toward the shallower water. I heard the peeler run was on a week earlier causing the rockfish to feed more toward shore on soft crabs then on alewives in the deeper water.

I guessed right because as soon as we hit 29 feet of water one of my deep lines went off. Frank, also known as "Rod Hog", was the first to react and grabbed the rod. It was a beauty! 31 inches was called out as Frank took it off the measuring board. I continued my western trek and I saw Henry jump up and grab the starboard dummy line. Just before he grabbed the line I saw that the bungee cord was tight with the main line. I knew that this had to be a good one since the bungee stayed so tight against the main line. I was right, 32-3/4 inches on the measuring board. By the time we hit 27-foot of water we had several other lines go off. All of the fish thus far were well over the 18 inch minimum.

For the first time this year, I could really read a tremendous amount of fish in a given area. In fact, it was so good that I saw a huge school of fish on my depth finder and told my crew to get ready for some action. Shortly after they disappeared off of my depth finder screen my three dummy lines were being stretched to their limits. As three of my crew grabbed each one of them, my two center rods, which are my deep rods, bent in half. Shortly after that, two of my long lines had fish pulling out drag from the reel. Luckily, there was enough time for Ron and John to bring in the dummy lines, put the fish in the fish box and grab the last two long lines that went off.

Needless to say there was a *"helluva"* mess on the back deck of my boat. It must have taken 15 minutes to get all of the lines straightened out and back in the water. Unfortunately, all of the fish we were catching did not go into the fish box. There were many sub-legal fish of 16 to 17-7/8 inches.

After three hours we had our limit of rockfish ranging from 20 inches to almost 33 inches. What a day! It was one of those days that you dream about. It was one of those days that you wanted everyone you knew to be onboard. Several times we had multiple reels screaming with fish, while the dummy lines were being stretched to their max. WHAT A TRIP!

A FUN DAY OF FISHING ON THE CHESAPEAKE BAY

Fishing has been fantastic since the onset of the rockfish season on April 20th. The first half was the best that I can recall for catching large stripers. On May 16th, Maryland initiated their second phase of the striped bass season. Anglers had a possession limit of only one fish over a 28 inch minimum size limit during the first part of the season. During the second segment of the fishery, anglers were allowed to keep two fish over an 18 inch minimum size limit.

Since fishing was still awesome through the middle of July, I called a few of my fishing buddies to set a date. Saturday, July 19th was workable for everyone. On Friday evening, I picked up a frozen four-gallon bucket of chum, a box of whole menhaden for bait as well as two gallons of razor clams. I kept the chum and bait in my truck in a cooler overnight. Believe it or not the chum was still frozen solid Saturday morning. Igloo coolers are great!

I arrived at the marina at 5:30 a.m., unloaded my truck and grabbed a cart and wheeled it down to my boat after getting 40 pounds of ice for the fish box and my personal cooler. After loading everything in my boat, Jim and Ron showed up with a couple of coolers of their own. Finally at 6 a.m. Tim and Terry arrived to fulfill my crew for the day. After warming the engines for a few minutes, the dock lines were cast off and we were heading out of the slip. As we passed number 1 marker, I put the boat up on plane. Our target was the Summer Gooses, 12 miles away. Forty minutes later, we were at our destination.

There must have been more than 20 boats anchored on the Gooses by the time we arrived. I surveyed the area with my depth finder to see if I could find some fish to anchor on. Ten minutes later, I saw a few fish near the bottom in 21 feet of water. I sent Terry up to the bow to lower the anchor. While Terry was setting the anchor, Tim and Ron were handing the rods out to Jim from the cabin. After Terry told me that the anchor was set, I turned off the engines and grabbed the chum bucket. I immediately started slinging the ground up menhaden overboard. Ron got out the cutting board and placed the metal rod into a rod holder. Tim grabbed a couple of baits out of the cooler with two hands full of razor clams. Placing them on the cutting board, Tim started to cut up the menhaden.

I was using 5/0 circle hooks in order to be able to release undersize stripers without harming them. We had 10 rods set with either cut bait or razor clams. We sat back and left the rods in the rod holders. Before you knew it, one of the rods showed a fish taking the bait. Within a few seconds the rod was bent in half. Tim jumped from his seat and grabbed the rod before I could say *"fish on"*. As the fish neared the boat, I grabbed the net and slid a 29 inch rockfish into the net. After exchanging *"high fives"* and a couple of pictures, the fish went in the fish box.

Wow! What a way to start the day. Most of the rockfish being caught here were in the 20 to 22 inch range. Several minutes later we had a double header with a nice pair of stripers pulling on our lines. Both measured 20 inches and were quickly put in the box. After a few undersized rockfish, Ron grabbed a bent rod and said he had a monster on. Ron spent what seemed like 10 minutes going from one side of the boat to the other. The fish was strong and took line at will off the drag. I grabbed the net as the fish neared. In the back of my mind I knew what was on Ron's line, but I didn't want to say anything. However, my inkling was right as the fish broke the surface with its wings flapping violently. Yes, it was a cownose ray that we quickly cut from our line before he could tangle any more lines. Needless to say, we teased Ron the rest of the day about his monster.

Three hours later we were pulling anchor and had ten nice rockfish in the box. The first fish of the day turned out to be the largest of the day. Our catch consisted of stripers from 18 inches to 29 inches with the bulk of them averaging around 20 inches.

It was a beautiful day on the Chesapeake Bay with temperatures in the 80's and a light breeze out of the south. Catching those stripers on light tackle just made the day perfect. Everyone had a great time and we are planning another chumming trip in late August. I'm hoping that the fish will be just as cooperative.

 # FISHING ON ELECTION DAY

It was Tuesday, November 7th, Election Day for our Nation. After three straight weekends in a row with winds pushing over the 20-knot mark, weather forecasters predicted light southerly winds for Tuesday. Jerry booked this trip with me several months ago knowing he would have the day off due to the fact that it was Election Day and he is a school teacher. Jerry invited three other teachers and two of his friends to fish with him.

Jerry and crew met me at the boat at 6:30 a.m. After introductions and stowing their gear in the cabin we were out of the slip heading south. It took us 40 minutes to arrive at our destination, which was a mile or so above the Calvert Cliffs Power Plant. We started trolling in

48 feet of water as I played out the lines. I put out a spread of eleven rods containing a variety of lures. I was using the same size lures that I used in the spring rockfish fishery. Large 10/0 bucktails, parachutes up to 20 ounces and umbrella rigs were my lures of choice. White was my color preference but I did have yellow and chartreuse just in case they wanted something different.

In addition to my eleven rods, I also used three dummy lines. All of my lines are double rigged, which meant that I was pulling a combination of 28 different lures behind my boat. After deploying my rods, I then put out my dummy lines. As I was putting out my second dummy line, I explained to the crew exactly how they work. I have a bungee cord attached to my nylon line. Because of the way that I have it tied, the nylon line will have a loop in the line where I attach it to my stern cleat. Pulling the bungee cord out causes the nylon line to come even with the bungee cord. As I was putting out my last dummy line, one of the crew hollered that the starboard dummy line was being straightened out. Knowing that a fish was on the other end tugging, I told Gil to bring in the hand line. After netting it and placing it on the measuring board, it was 36 inches in length. Wow! What a way to start the day! A beauty in the box in less than fifteen minutes of fishing.

It took another hour to produce another striper. This time it hit a 10/0 white bucktail on a four-arm umbrella rig out 150 feet from the boat. It measured 27 inches and was quickly put into the fish box. One of the guys, I won't say who, was a real clock-watcher and informed me that it was close to another hour when the port-side rod started to scream. Doug picked it up and started to battle. A short while later a 33-inch rockfish was going into the box.

As the noon hour was approaching, the bay couldn't have gotten any nicer with flat, calm seas. It was a real pleasure to be able to fish in conditions like this, rather than those four footers we had on Sunday. The clock-watcher again informed me that another hour was about to pass and we were due for another fish. Within five minutes, the middle transom rod went off. I had two large bucktails on this rod and knew that it had to be a nice size fish to inhale one of these baits. After a 10 minute battle, a 39 inch rockfish was placed in the box. It was now 1:30 p.m. and we had seven fish in the box, five of which were over 28 inches. We were only allowed one more fish over the 28 inch mark according to the state regulations governing the fishery. You

Jerry and The Beast

were allowed two fish per angler over 18 inches but only one of these could be over 28 inches.

As luck would have it, Jerry was standing by the port transom rod when it went off. This was no ordinary hit where a few feet of line was ripped off the reel. This was a magnificent hit as the lines started to be ripped off of the reel. You could see by the jerking of the rod that this huge fish was down there shaking its head trying to throw the lure. Leaving the helm, I came back to check the drag on the reel. I could tell that this was a monster of a fish by the way the line was stripping off the reel and the constant bend in the rod. I tried to slow the boat to ease the pressure as I started to turn to the port to help Jerry keep the fish on the outside of the boat. By now, Jerry was pumping the rod to gain a few feet only to have the fish pull off another foot. Eventually, Jerry started to gain on the beast, as the fish was now 25 feet behind the boat. I grabbed the net and after getting a good look at the rockfish I knew I was in trouble. Now the fish is within 10 feet of the boat and it is huge. The umbrella rig was attached directly to the line so Jerry had to work the fish up to the boat with his rod in order for me to net it. Now is the time for Murphy's Law to come into play. First, the free bucktail of this tandem rig gets tangled in the net and keeps me from scooping the net under the fish. Next, the fish swims under the dummy line, then back on top of it getting entangled in the process. Now, I had the net and swooped down only to get its head and a third of his body in the net, yet he was still entangled in the dummy line. I tried raising the net but the huge fish fell out of it while still dangling on the dummy line. Jerry, knowing that he is about to lose the biggest fish he has ever caught, jumps over the railing and onto the swim platform. Jerry reached down, held on to the railing with one hand and grabbed the fish through the gills and heaved it over the rail onto the deck. With one last head-shake the fish broke the line and the lure fell from its mouth.

Since this was our limit for fish over 28 inches, I suggested that we stop trolling for rockfish. There was no need to kill one of these magnificent beauties for any reason. We had eight legal rockfish in the box and still had some time remaining for our trip.

Knowing of the seatrout in the area, I suggested we break out the spinning rods and jig for seatrout.

Moving north, we came across a couple dozen seagulls working over breaking fish. I eased the boat up-tide of the birds and allowed myself to drift through the area. By this time, as I stopped the forward motion of the boat, everyone opened the bales of their reels and quickly dropped their lures to the bottom. With two jerks of the rod tip, Gil had hooked up. Within a second, two more until all six anglers had seatrout pulling on their rods.

Within a second two more until all six anglers had seatrout pulling on their rods. Gil's rod stayed bent until I reached over to net two four-pound seatrout. Once again I had double rigged my lines. During that first pass, nine trout were brought on board and six of them found their way to the box.

The birds moved a 100 feet north and started to work again. We followed and the same scenario occurred. Six rods went down and seatrout from 12 to 27 inches. This lasted another 15 minutes before the seagulls broke up and went in search of other breaking fish.

We continued heading north and stopped at several locations where seagulls were setting on the water. Quite often seagulls will sit where the fish were breaking in hopes that they will begin to work again in the area. Most of these gulls were working in water of 60 to 90 feet. We were using small bucktails of yellow and chartreuse, stingsilvers and crippled herrings. All caught just as good as the next one.

A glimpse of the watch and the lack of tide, I suggested that we call it a day. It was 3:00 and still bright and sunny with a mild 65 degree temperature as we headed for port. Arriving back at the docks, the crew helped unload the catch of eight rockfish and 35 seatrout and placed them in a cart to wheel them to the fish cleaning station. I was curious on exactly how big Jerry's fish was, so I asked him to put it on the weigh scale. I was astonished to hear that it weighed 49 pounds.

What a beast! What a trip! What a fall fishery!

STRIPER FISHING IN NOVEMBER

It was the first of the week when I went to the marine weather site on my computer. I was planning to fish the entire weekend, Friday, Saturday and Sunday of November 22nd. NOAA was predicting light winds out of the southwest for Friday but they were calling for a gale of 20 to 30 knot winds out of the north for Saturday. Finally, on Thursday of that week they predicted the wind direction to change course and come out of the northwest. This was somewhat encouraging but I was not thrilled about fishing in those conditions. Fortunately, I was fishing out of the Rod & Reel Dock in Chesapeake Beach and knew that the western shore would provide me with some protection.

My party was composed of the Moore brothers and four of their friends. They met at the scheduled time of 6:30 a.m. I noticed that they did not bring any bags or coolers with them. After a hello they asked me if we were still going fishing. A look at the local flagpole showed that the flag was waving straight out of the northwest. I said that if they wanted to try it that we may be able to get the day in if we stayed fairly close to the western shore. Chris Moore told me that they were really looking forward to going and they would go back to their vehicles to grab their gear and coolers.

By 7:00 a.m. we were casting off our dock lines and leaving the slip. Turning to the weather channel on the marine VHF radio it announced that the winds were out of the northwest at 27 knots and gusting up to 32 knots at the Thomas Point Lighthouse. We headed east out of the Rod & Reel Dock to the #1 day marker. The previous day I had limited out on rockfish up to 36 inches just north outside of Herring Bay. Knowing that the western shore would provide me some protection, I opted to turn south and look for rockfish near the Radar Screen to Parker's Creek.

Although it was blowing a gale, as long as we stayed within 30 to 35 foot contour line off of the shore we only had two-foot chop. As soon as you went an additional quarter mile toward the east and got into 40 foot of water the waves quickly built to four to five feet. Needless to say, we stayed in the 30 foot water depth the remainder of the day.

A few charterboats left before we did and were already trolling from the Radar Screen down to Breezy Point. We laid out our seven lines trying to keep the lures in the correct strike zone near the bottom. We worked our way south from where we started at the Radar Screen. Going in and out from 35 foot to 27 foot looking for stripers on the depth finder. Although we did see several schools of rockfish on the meter, they were not interested in our offerings. We did manage to have a collision with a striper of 18-1/2 inches, which we quickly put in the box after an hour of trolling. There was no question about keeping this fish because of the weather. You never want to look a gift horse in the mouth.

By 10:00 we had made our way down to outside of Breezy Point Marine. At that time, we had two rockfish in the cooler and I was getting a little worried about the remainder of the day. The wind was still howling through the boat at about 30 knots and we only had two fish. However, it was still very fishable even with that much wind. It did make it very uncomfortable when we had to turn our stern to the wind. In fact, it was downright cold! As we were still working southward, I finally saw seagulls working over breaking fish. I picked up speed in order to close the distance fast before the birds stopped working. Slowing down as I approached the birds, I looked around to see if any other boats were in the area. They weren't! We  had them all to ourselves. As we made our first pass, I watched the depth finder fill up with rockfish all over the bottom. Turning around to watch my rods I saw the first fish hit my 330 GTI Penn combo outfit. The fish pulled it down hard as the drag system started to scream. Within seconds, two more rods went off with rockfish tugging at their drag systems.

Three stripers up to 36 inches went into the cooler. I hurried to get the lines back in the water and to make a turn to go back to the fish. Before I had a chance to turn the wheel, I noticed another large group of birds working ahead of me. I opted to fish that group of birds instead of turning around. It was a good choice. Again I saw stripers on the meter as we circled the birds. Before I had a chance to turn around to watch my rods I heard "fish on". Seconds later, I saw another rod being bent in half. By the time we got those two fish in the boat we had another fish hit my outside port rod. The hit was so hard I though it was going to pull my rod holder overboard. It was a brute of 39 inches and was quickly deposited into the fish box.

Although the bird action did not last that long, we still managed to get our limit of 12 stripers and one additional one for the boat. Luckily, I had a GPS/plotter system onboard, which keeps track of my boat path. All I had to do was to follow my path back to the fish. It worked every time and by 11:30 we were rolling up our lines as we were preparing for the bumpy ride home.

It turned out to be a fantastic day. Yes, it was a little chilly but as soon as we got into the fish, things really warmed up and you forgot about the cold. This was fall fishing at its best. So if you put your boat away before November, you are missing out on some of the best action Maryland has to offer. The thrill of catching a striped bass over 36 inches is worth tolerating a little bit of cold weather. I fished two days later on Monday, November 25th with no jacket, only my long sleeve shirt because it was so mild. Remember all you have to do is dress properly for the weather. Listen to the weather forecast to pick your days of mild weather.

Even if you put your boat away for the winter in September or October you can still get out to fish on a charterboat. Book them mid-November to the 15th of December for the best action if you are looking for a trophy rockfish.

THE FISHING TRIP TO REMEMBER

May 10th was the day that I was looking forward to since the MSSA Annual Convention in February, which was held at the Princess Royale Suites in Ocean City. During the convention MSSA auctioned off three fishing trips to the highest bidders. George Wendling was bidding on the "*Spring Trophy Rockfish*" trip that I donated to the MSSA. As the bid was going on, George stated that he was bidding on the trip for all the girls in his party. It was seven young, lovely ladies sitting at the two tables that were reserved for George since he won the "*Overall Captain of the Year*" from the MSSA for the 2002 fishing season! George brought his own fan club.

As luck would be smiling on me that night, George made the final bid on the trip. Wow! Was I delighted?! Right away I had three guys offer to be my first mate for the day. I wasn't having any part of sharing this trip with those hungry wolves. At the conclusion of the auction, I went over and thanked George for his winning bid and told the girls that I was looking forward to taking them out for a day of fishing on the Bay.

George called me a couple of months later and we set the date for the trip, May 10th. Lisa, George's wife, was the first to arrive at the boat. She told me that the rest of the girls were in the parking lot gathering their gear and would be here shortly. Lisa went back to the parking lot to show the girls the way. Well, let me tell you what a spectacle that turned out to be. All seven girls had bright yellow sweatshirts on as they pushed two carts loaded with a couple of coolers of beer and baggage. They immediately gave me a similar yellow sweatshirt with my boat name embroidered on it. It looked great and I put it on immediately. I still had to fight off several more wolves (captains) on the dock trying to get onboard. What a sight we must have made as we pulled out of the Rod & Reel Dock at Chesapeake Beach!

The girls were on time and by 6:45 we stowed everything away and were pulling out of the slip. By the time we reached #1 marker I could hear that familiar sound of beer cans being opened. Yes, they said that this was going to be a fun day. After motoring out to the 35 foot contour line off of the Radar Screen, we slowed the boat and started trolling.

I assigned several of the girls different task to help as we began fishing. Two of the girls, Donna and Chris, unraveled the line off of the planer boards. As that job was completed we deployed the boards. As I was letting out the correct amount of line on each reel, I had Janet ready with the rubber bands and clips as Leigh was in charge of grabbing the planer board line. Oh, I forgot to mention that Lisa was driving the boat and didn't even hit another boat. I then had three of the girls unravel the dummy lines. Twenty minutes later we had 13 rods and 3 dummy lines in the water. Within an hour the first rod went off. Screams erupted from the girls as Janet was given the rod. She did a great job fighting the fish. How we were able to capture this fish without tangling the other lines was a miracle. As I was helping Janet fight the fish, Rosemary was at the helm while Robin was manning the net. Everything went perfectly and we landed a healthy 39-inch rockfish as more screams were heard across the Bay. Little did we know that this was going to be the biggest fish of the day.

As the day went on we were able to put several more nice stripers in the box. During the lull between fish these girls could hold three different conversations with one another and knew what each person was discussing. What a racket! Every time  we had a *"hook up"* the girls would scream. Every time we landed a fish the girls would scream. Talk about being excited over a fish! Of course every time we caught a fish it was time to celebrate with another Coors Light. At other times throughout the day, when we weren't catching any fish, the girls would try singing to entice the fish to hit.

The girls brought plenty of finger foods such as celery, carrots, broccoli and dip, grapes and strawberries, and sandwiches with chip and pretzels. By 2:00 p.m. we had seven trophy rockfish in the fish box and two empty 30 packs of Coors Light. We then headed back to the dock.

The girls were real troopers as they tolerated a heavy downpour of rain throughout the morning and a northeast wind at 18 knots. By mid-day the sun came out and the winds subsided. It did turn out to be a great fishing trip

BOOK ORDER FORM

I would like to order _____ copies of *Catchin' Chesapeake Rockfish*

Number of copies _____ x $19.95 each = $ _____

Maryland Residents:
    Add $1.00 Sales Tax per book   =   + _____

Shipping & Handling:
    Add $4.00 per book   =   + _____

           TOTAL ENCLOSED: $ _____

Make checks payable to: Chesapeake Sportfishing
                            PO Box 643
                            Pasadena, MD 21123

Ship to: _____
                            Name

_____
                        Street Address

_____
      City   State   Zip Code

Phone: _____

Bulk purchase inquiries invited: Call 410-686-3463

Only Mastercard and Visa Accepted:

Expiration Date: | | | |